Seeing the World Through New Eyes

By

Usman Kadir

with

Daniel Roberts

A journey from extremism to love

Published by Vivid Publishing
P.O. Box 948, Fremantle
Western Australia 6959
www.vividpublishing.com.au

National Library of Australia Cataloguing-in-Publication data:

Author: Kadir, Usman, author.
Title: Seeing my world through new eyes : a journey from extremism
            to love / Usman Kadir, Daniel Roberts.
ISBN: 9781922204325 (paperback)
Subjects: Kadir, Usman,
            Christian converts from Islam--Biography.
            Islam--Relations--Christianity.
            Christianity and other religions--Islam.
Other Authors/Contributors:
            Roberts, Daniel John, author.
Dewey Number: 248.246092

Seeing the World Through New Eyes

A journey from extremism to love

Preface

U sman Kadir has impacted an increasing number of Christians over the past few years with his message. I have personally been greatly encouraged by him. He has become known as the 'Smiling Imam', with his favourite verse in Scripture "It is finished" (John 19:30). Through Jesus, he has had a heart transformation from a life of imparting terror, to a life of imparting love.

The first section of this book was particularly painful for Usman to write. To do so, he had to revisit over 40 years of his life where he shares how he "spent my life circulating hatred towards the name of Jesus." As such, the first section in this book has numerous references to Christians as "pagans". This is written in the context of Usman Kadir's paradigm of his former life, and we have avoided using this term in inverted commas each time this word is used to avoid repetition.

Most of the first two sections of this book are narrative, with Usman telling his story of living under modern *Sharia* Law. These sections detail the complete paradigm shift Usman experienced. He explains that "Now, I can only look ahead with a new message." The following two sections explain the context of *Sharia* Law, its parallels with the Torah, as well as Christ coming to bring a solution for the human heart.

As you read Sections 2 and 3, you will realise that there is a very different set of 'History Books' between the Christian and Muslim world. In one sense, this book is endeavouring to help the reader view history through the eyes of a Muslim who has experienced a heart transformation. While the traditional view that most Christians hold to concerning Islam remains, it is difficult for the love that Jesus brought to be extended to the descendants of Ishmael.

Some may be confused after the change in Usman's life how he can still be a leader and Imam within Islam. Hopefully this will become clearer later in this book. Beyond that, can I suggest another book written by Usman and three other Muslim leaders that will provide further clarity concerning many of the questions Christians may have. Titled *The Family I Never Knew I Had,* this can be purchased at: www.ancient-ties-restored.com . You can read the first chapter of this book in the Appendix of *Seeing the World Through New Eyes.*

From before the time of the New Testament's writing, the Eastern and Western worlds have experienced a *"dividing wall of hostility"* as explained by Paul in Ephesians 2:14. The vision of Paul was that, in Christ, the two shall become one. That is, East and West, Muslim and Christian, becoming one family.

As Usman Kadir says, it is time to stop being suspicious of one another, and embrac truth. This is the path that Usman has taken. I invite you to take a step toward understanding a little more of this culture and faith by sharing in the incredible journey and message of this man.

Daniel Roberts

Introduction:

For many of you reading this book, your world may look very different to mine. The responsibility that God has given me in this life is to be an educator of the Islamic peoples. This may be preaching during Friday prayers, teaching at numerous *Maddrasah's*, or leading smaller groups with study from the Holy *Qur'an*. However, you should also know that there is still much we share in common.

As we look over our lives, there are often several events we can point to that profoundly alter the course of our life from that moment on. For me, one such event occurred as a 6-month-old baby, when I was removed from my biological parents to be raised by my adoptive parents, who lived thousands of miles away.

It was a move from a multi-cultural community, to a household where I was raised to live under *Sharia* Law – a very different life to that of the majority of Muslims. However this was the world that I would accept as reality. It was the only world I knew, the only way of living I was presented with, for most of my life.

This life under *Sharia* Law meant that I was to be 'God's instrument' in extending His rule in my nation. This meant that I was to remove 'pagan' Christians from the territory where Muslims resided – by force if necessary. It included closing pagan bars selling alcohol. All this was seen as a contamination of the standards mankind was to live by under the God of Abraham. We saw the ultimate threat of paganism as being through the influence of the West, and that had to be resisted!

This was the belief I was taught to embrace, and the way I saw my world. One day that would all be shaken.

I would see my world through new eyes.

Part 1:

Living Under Sharia

Chapter 1:
The seeds are planted...

As a six-month-old baby, my biological parents took me to another island to be raised by a different family. The reason for this was that my place of birth was predominantly Christian, and my parents desired for me to be raised as someone obedient to Islam. They believed their relatives on this island could do that – away from the harmful influences of paganism, Westernism and Christianity. This geographical shift as a six-month-old set the direction of the next 40 years of my life.

I was born in a predominantly Muslim nation, however with a growing acceptance of Western culture, particularly in urban settings. From the viewpoint of my village, the Western influence on urban life was having negative affects upon Muslim youth, leading to the consumption of alcohol and immoral living. This was the effect of Christianity in my nation. The village I was raised in however was simple, yet isolated from much of these influences.

Since the days when I was a young child, my extended family, my (non-biological) parents, and my community planted a view of life that I was to be a Muslim who needed to be obedient according to God's laws. I was raised understanding that Islamic Law was an obligation to be kept by mankind. As a child, I embraced the beliefs that my parents taught me. I didn't understand the true meaning of Islamic faith; it was simply the world I was born into. To me, Islam was God's blessing for the world to follow.

Growing up, I was intrigued by the Christian village across the other side of the fast-flowing, large river that divided our lives. Sometimes we went onto the river in small boats and fished together with the children from the Christian village. My parents told me not to become too close to them, as they were pork-eating pagans. The Christian village was only 500 metres away, including the river that separated us. However, the greater divide between our lives was over 1,000 years of tradition.

What was particularly intriguing to me was the western family that lived in this neighbouring Christian village. To me as a five-year-old child, they seemed to be very friendly. Often when we had problems with major sickness or other issues they would cross over by their boat and be there to help. Although their beliefs and practices were unwelcome in my village, their help and assistance was usually gratefully accepted. The western missionaries across the river were good examples of people who helped those like us, who didn't always have the means to cope with life's challenges. For example, when there was a medical emergency they would often transport our village members on their boat up the river to the nearest hospital.

Growing up as a young child, I would often be given the task of doing the prayer call in my village mosque. With its loud speakers at the top of the minaret directed towards the Christian village across the river, I am not sure my Arabic prayer call was always appreciated!

Obedience to Islam was the ultimate goal in life. This was the world I lived in. This was the world I was proud of. There were few outside influences to challenge or expand my thinking, and consequently, I had no ideas contrary to what my parents, extended family and community taught me.

As a young child, I grew up understanding the obligations of Islam by the thorough and strict instruction of my parents. Obedience to Islam begins within the household. I was taught in my home how to read the *Qur'an*[1] in Arabic to a very high standard. Within my household, we would have a *Qur'anic*

---

[1] *Muslims believe that the Qur'an was revealed from God through the Angel Gabriel to the Prophet Muhammad. This revelation occurred throughout the Prophet Muhammad's lifetime, in the early 7th Century, and is the central Holy Book of modern Islam.*

reading schedule both for me, my brothers and sisters, as well as my friends. At every available moment, whether at a spontaneous or a pre-set time, I would be tested in my *Qur'anic* reading ability by my parents. We would sit on the floor with the Qur'an on a reading stand or small pillow, passing the Qur'an to the next person when it was their turn to read. My parents would call out "repeat it again", if ever I recited the reading with incorrect Arabic pronunciation.

Although we spoke our national language at home, we would never see a Qur'an with a translation into my everyday language - we would only recite from an Arabic *Qur'an*, until I became fluent in its foundational texts. These texts were shorter Arabic verses, with my speed and fluency being observed by my parents at each recitation. I was tested over many months and years as a young child, not only in regards to my speed and fluency, but also in my ability to memorize the *Qur'an* without the text in front of me. Beyond instruction in my family environment, as a young child I was also obligated to attend religious classes.

Receiving religious education at home was a highly disciplined practice. If I was not developing according to my parents' expectations they would get angry and I was beaten. This might be with the broom in the corner or with the cane that was always ready on hand to bring correction. I sometimes left my lessons with a red and raw backside. The hope of my parents was that my religious discipline would always be greater than that of the community around me. According to the understanding they had inherited, the obedience of their son to God's Laws contributed towards their own salvation.

Each morning, I would be required to get up between 3am to 3:30am. The early start was so I could begin the day with morning prayers, *sholat*[2] *Subuh*, the first of five daily prayer rituals. Rarely

[2] *Muslims are obligated to do 5 prayers called Sholat throughout the day. This begins with Sholat Subuh usually prior to 5am, with the final prayer being Sholat Isya . Usually Sholat Maghrib, prayed just after sunset, is the most diligently observed by most Muslims. The Sholat parallels the prayer form in the Old Testament by Jews. (See Nehemiah 8:6)*

did I sleep in; if this happened I faced the anger of my parents. I was somewhat free from my parents' supervision at 7am when they departed for their work activities. Before parting ways, we would *sholat* together as a family in our lounge room at the same time, and then everyone would go their separate ways for their day's activities. At *Maghrib*, the early evening prayer, we would come together as a family after my parents returned home from work to *sholat*, and continue in our *Qur'an*ic recitation. After *sholat Magrib*, typically some friends would come over to my house to improve our recitation and memorization ability, coming because my parents were considered teachers in recitation. Nearly every day, this would be the routine of my life.

It seems that Islamic children in this present era are brought up in a different lifestyle and culture than the era in which I was raised. For my village in particular, and especially for my family, training children was a very authoritarian practice. In contrast to this, I see whilst Arabic recitation is still taking place in many Muslim homes, children are often doing traditional dancing in the lounge room, or playing on their electronic games! This stands in stark contrast to my upbringing, where I would be harshly disciplined for shortcomings such as incorrectly reciting the *Qur'an* – and in such a way that it would regularly result in bleeding from head wounds.

As a young child, the desire to be more independent like other children I saw was certainly felt within my heart. However, it didn't occur to me that I lived under strong discipline - I thought it was normal. In fact, this was genuine Islamic practice, as far as I understood. I wanted to be the best I could be in following the laws of Islam. As such, the dominant priorities within my life as a child were the disciplines of *sholat*, followed by *Qur'anic* recitation. Attending Friday prayers, which are attended by Muslims all around the world in their local mosque, was also a non-negotiable. In fact, I usually prayed at the front of the mosque with my father, as he wanted to display his son as someone growing in spiritual awareness and obedience.

However, I was still a young child at heart, testing the borders of my parents' patience. I remember one particular moment when there were a number of friends doing the *sholat* in front of me in the mosque, bending over at the 90 degree position preparing to kneel. The temptation for a six-year-old was too much, and I pushed my nearest friend over as he was doing the *sholat*, causing a chain reaction of young friends losing their balance. After going home I was beaten by my father, and knew I would never do that again!

The obligations of *Sharia* law[3] are for people over the age of seven years old. Below seven, children are not considered accountable for their actions, and if they die their sins are not held against them. However above seven years old, *Sharia* requires the individual to follow Islamic Law in order to be obedient to God. This understanding pushes parents, and certainly pushed my own parents, to pursue the raising of a child who would be in right standing with God through the practice of strict religious disciplines.

During the main hours of the day I studied in the government elementary school. After finishing studies there at 1pm, I would go straight to the *Madrassah*[4] to continue religious education and *Qur'anic* recitation along with other children from our village. There we would learn a number of new things concerning the Islamic religious service, as well as the pillars of the Islamic faith. Attendance at the *Madrassah* was nearly every day, from 1 pm to 4 pm. This was my life from 8 years old, continuing into my teenage years.

---

[3] *Sharia Law is the moral code and religious law of Islam. It is often a controversial subject within Islam, as it applies the Law of early Islam in modern societies. Generally most Muslims practice parts of Sharia Law that are adaptable to modern society, whilst some countries attempt to be governed as a nation under Sharia Law in its entirety.*

[4] *A Madrassah is an Islamic Boarding School*

Despite the disciplined religious instruction, I still found time during any free moments I had to play games with spinning tops, or other simple games that would capture the imagination. I would be particularly excited when the time of year for Ramadan (the fasting month) arrived. I was taught that Ramadan is a glorious month. As the sunset occurred and the fasting of both food and liquid was finished for the day, everything tasted so much better! Each night there were special services in the mosque that we would attend. The feasting in the evening and late nights of games, especially during the completion of the fasting month, called Idul Fitri, made this time one of the year's highlights.

Within our village, there were no Christian minorities who lived among us. The closest we came to paganism was when one of us boys didn't sholat for two days, in which case someone would call out, "You pagan!" Our neighbourhood was renowned and honoured in our region for its commitment to Islamic tradition. There were still people within the village who would leave and get good jobs in banks and other private companies, however within my family, it was the following of Islamic Law which was truly honoured. This meant a commitment to such things as a *Halal* diet, fasting for the month of *Ramadhan,* and ensuring that women would wear full head covering when leaving the home.

At 12 years of age, I received special additional Islamic education. At the beginning, I did not know what this type of education was for - all I knew was it was important for me to understand and practice as a Muslim. In this special education, we learnt that Islam needed to be embraced by all people and nations. Prior to this, growing up as a child, my understanding of Islam was that it was a personal discipline.

As I approached my teenage years, the education I received both at home and at the *Madrassah* began to develop a deep commitment to a specific mandate within Islam. This mandate was to outwork *Sharia* Law; to live so that other areas would reflect the obedience to Islamic Law that we observed within our own neighbourhood.

As I looked across the river and saw the Christian village that did not live according to the traditions of Islam, I used to wonder as a child how I could enjoy playing their games. Now as a teenager, I was wondering how they could become like us.

From the son of a Missionary, living across the River:

As the son of a western missionary, I spent much of my childhood across the river from Usman Kadir. I was about 10 years younger than Usman. The ethnic group on my side of the river was very different from the devout Muslim community Usman grew up with.

Amazingly, the Bible message was a part of my side of the river for more than 50 years, yet the Muslims across the river had probably never heard the Gospel, except for the brief interactions they had with my family. The people in our village had no understanding of the Muslim people, nor did the Muslims understand us! They would wonder how we survived without going fishing every day, as their primary income was through fishing and agriculture. I heard many strange stories from the Muslim village about how they thought we made money out of nothing, like a magic snake that produced gold on demand!

As someone who grew up from infancy in this remote area, I was one of the few people from my village who over time developed close contact with the Muslim village. As an adventurous seven-year-old, I was quite fascinated by them, and began to work together with them in a variety of ways as I grew up. Looking back, I believe God was bringing me on a journey where the divide between Muslims and myself would no longer be an obstacle.

In the last five years that I lived in that village I entered my teenage years. I became more independent, and my interaction with the Muslim village changed significantly. As a young man, I started a small gold mining operation with two young men from the Muslim village, and I was also playing sport with their village two or three times a week. As my interactions with this village increased, I developed levels of friendship that overlooked differences.

I began to hunt regularly with my friends from the Muslim village. I had some good dogs that helped with chasing down deer, and my Muslim friends could see that they were useful, although they were somewhat scared of the dogs. They would call me to cross the river when they saw deer nearby, and we would work together on the hunt.

Throughout these years I would usually take the canoe across the river to their village. However as the Muslim youths became more comfortable with me, they started to come over to my village and visit my house. They would read books and were curious to find out more of our way of life. In fact a couple of youths (now grown up) still contact me on Facebook. Looking back, it was fascinating to see how the enormous differences we perceived in our childhood ceased to matter as much over time.

As a young child, I would hear the Muslim youths doing the prayer call in Arabic. Their voices were clearly heard across the river. A young man called Usman Kadir was one of the regular enthusiastic youths doing the call to prayer. We would have a very different life journey, but our paths would meet again decades later.

Chapter 2:
The foundations for Sharia Law are formed

As a young teenager, my life was firmly entrenched in Islamic education, where Islamic law needed to be not only understood, but fully obeyed. It was a unique life within Islam for me, as compared to most other Muslims in many other parts of the world. As a teenager, I entered a transitional phase where I could more actively proclaim the belief I had embraced, the belief that I was proud of. I believed I was a Muslim who was moving towards perfect Islam, and everything outside of that perfect Islam was pagan. The perfect law was clearly planted within my life, and I considered that those who were pagan could not be approached, as they were unclean. I needed to remove myself from them, and remove them from the territory where Islam existed.

I was proud as a Muslim, and with youthful passion I adopted the goal, dream and desire that Islam would be cleansed from all that is impure. I was filled with enthusiasm and boldness to bring about the perfect law of Islam. This was my life growing up as a teenager. I embraced this way of seeing the world with my whole heart. During this time, we rarely heard the term *Injil*[5], or New Testament, even when reading the *Qur'an*. We would focus on the texts in the *Qur'an* that were not dealing with the *Injil*, or the other Holy Books embraced by the pagans.

By the time I reached 15 years of age, my parents felt they had raised me on the straight and narrow path and that I'd become a young man passionate for truth. I was now ready to leave for the next phase of my preparation. I was to be sent overseas to a *Madrassah* in Malaysia, however this one was quite different from the one of my childhood. This was a boarding school that fully immersed me in training and implementing God's Holy Law for the next six years of my life.

---

[5]*The Arabic name for the New Testament*

My parents were proud of me and paid for this next stage in my education, so that my understanding of Islam would be better than those in my home village. When I arrived at the school in Malaysia, my initial thoughts were how modern and sophisticated the school was compared to my village training center. This boarding school had visiting speakers who would captivate me with their information, compared to the routine memorisation I learned back in my home village.

All the training within the *Madrassah* was focused upon understanding Islamic Law. We were imprisoned in a particular teaching and mindset, which contrasts strongly to my later approach to *Qur'anic* study of understanding the original context of each verse. The mindset that increasingly developed in the *Madrassah* was that we were obedient to the law and moving towards perfection, while the rest of the world was appearing increasingly pagan.

After arriving in the Islamic Boarding School in Malaysia, we were taught about the Holy Books of the Old and New Testament (Taurat, Zabur, Injil). Although these books are spoken of throughout the *Qur'an*, and in fact are one of the official pillars of our Islamic faith, it was taught clearly by our teacher that these books cannot be trusted, that they've been altered. I was told that they've been altered by the pagans themselves: Jews and Christians. Therefore, we cannot place our faith in these books. There was a lot of new information for me to absorb in this time.

At the boarding school, we were encouraged to destroy these Holy Books if ever we came across them. Whenever we read about the Holy Books in the *Qur'an*, we read those verses with this new understanding. To desire to understand the contents of the Old and New Testament was *haram*[6], that is forbidden – it was an unclean desire. The only true Holy Book was the *Qur'an*.

---

[6]*An Arabic term meaning "forbidden"*

A journey from extremism to love

Following this growing understanding of the position of the Holy Books, as a teenager in training at 17 years old I genuinely viewed Christians as pagans and unclean. For me, together with my fellow boarding school students, this meant we would spit on them when they entered our territory. We were trying to pursue God's perfection, and when those who were pagan stepped into our territory, perfection couldn't be achieved. We would throw stones at the pagans if they were near our area. This was life for us, within a boarding school that pursued *Sharia* Law with fervency.

It was during this time that we prepared for a movement to bring the rule of Islam to the coastal areas of Malaysia. The ultimate goal was to have these coastal areas cleansed from pagans and the impurity that they brought.

I remember the excitement amongst the students as we were preparing to be sent out as Jihadists. This did not necessarily mean in a military sense at this time. That would come later. We would fast together, and all our education became a foundation for this movement in bringing communities to conform to Islam. For years we had recited and interpreted the Qur'an in regards to the pagan Christians, and how areas needed to be cleansed of paganism. Now it was time to put this into practice. I was ready to put my life on the line. There was an aggressive enthusiasm amongst myself and my peers, ready to pay a price - with our own blood if necessary - for our mandate to be fulfilled.

At that time, we didn't consider our Muslim brothers within Islam as pagan. We thought that anyone who was Muslim was good. This was based upon the *Hadith*[7], the sayings of the Prophet Muhammad, that you don't call your fellow Muslims pagan. But what was required of us was to call non-Muslims pagan. However, when non-Muslims spoke the confession to join the Islamic people, we would change our view of that person to be our close friend.

---

[7] *A collection of traditions containing sayings of the prophet Muhammad*

A journey from extremism to love

Seeing the World
Through New Eyes   19

All of this time, my parents were proud of me for pursuing an Islamic education, and I felt it was God's will for me to join this movement. Life in the *Madrassah* had a similar routine to that which I grew up with – such as getting up early for *Subuh, sholat.* But instead of going to a government school, it was 24 hours a day religious education. We had some English classes, however that was very limited. The interaction within the boarding school was almost entirely Arabic. Our whole lives were highly disciplined.

Previously in my younger years, I understood that Christians and Jews were pagans. This was simply information that I received and embraced. It was a less extreme view of non-Muslims. However, within the Islamic boarding school of my young adulthood, we were encouraged to develop an understanding that we had the right to *wage war* against pagans, that we had the right to invade and raid their possessions. These possessions, we believed, could rightly be utilised for the benefit of Muslims - those who were surrendered to God. Once we took these possessions, they were considered *halal* (clean). Maybe non-Muslims would be shocked at all of this; however at the time I believe that my enthusiasm and passion for perfection was desired by God.

Islam was to be the expression of the perfect, and because of that we needed to protect Islam from the imperfect. Therefore, all of these raids and invasions were to please our holy God, and to declare Islam so that mankind and their possessions could be made clean, according to perfect Islamic Law. I never stopped for a moment to contemplate that invasion and *jihad*[3] would be something that I would regret involvement with. On the contrary, I believed I was an instrument for the will of God. We verbalized continually the confession of the paganism of Christians. We understood that they endeavoured to bring paganism to Islam, to make us pagans. So our law was clear - oppose them, destroy them and drive them away. This was according to our

---

[8]*A war or struggle against unbelievers or the spiritual struggle within oneself against sin.*

understanding of our glorious *jihad* in bringing God's perfection to earth. When we proclaimed Christians as pagans, we were declaring a statement that was bringing us towards the purifying of society. The Christian pagans were bringing alcohol, *non-halal* diets and pornography to Muslim communities. It was our duty to purify our land of them.

Amongst many of the Islamic boarding schools, the understanding and paradigm taught was the same as that which we received. However, each school was independent of one another. All we knew was that we had a mandate, and that other Islamic boarding schools had a similar mandate, as part of a similar movement. We also grew to realize that we were different from other Muslims. We were the practitioners of *True Islam*. We were called to fully implement that which was revealed within the *Qur'an* and within the *Hadith*. This was the foundation for our movement.

Later we began to learn that within Islam itself there was paganism. This was a new stage of our mandate. We were to wage war against any form of Islam that reflected the practices of pagans. But in this case, we would try to strongly encourage our fellow Muslims to return to true Islam, and to embrace *Sharia* Law. This period within boarding school life where we became practitioners of 'true Islam' continued for six years. By 18 years old, during my last three years, we learnt to implement the *Sharia* movement. By 21 years old, I was regularly being sent out. The goal of being sent out was to change my nation to live under *Sharia* Law, the true Islam. However this was still on a local level, seeking to drive out those who would not live under Islamic Law in my local community.

I knew who my enemies were. The West was the primary example of paganism, the enemy of Islam, and the enemy of God's law. Therefore, we would send threats to those from the West. We also knew that our land was inhabited by missionaries, and they could not continue to be here. We would call the Western Christians dogs, pigs and other such names, particularly if they were living in Muslim areas.

Our goal was to remove Christians from our territory, as we couldn't be close to them or they would make us unclean. We generally didn't go looking for pagans, we just received the reports from our Muslim brothers and then go to their locations. Any pagan community needed to be removed. This would be done through throwing rocks and through abuse. These initial warnings, if not heeded, would then be followed by more extreme action. Within our boarding school there were about 250 students, and they would select the enthusiastic ones like me for these 'trips'. All of this time, my understanding was that I was implementing the will of God. I believed I was following truth.

Chapter 3:
Prepared for Holy Jihad

When I left the Boarding School in Malaysia for the Middle East to receive further training, I was being prepared to be a part of a movement. My purpose for leaving was so that my understanding of *Sharia* Law would be strengthened. I had formally finished my religious education in the *Madrassah* of my childhood; however I would continue to have close contact with them as they sent me out as an exemplary student and graduate, primed for additional training and instruction.

In a new country and somewhat new culture, I arrived in Pakistan to a training institution that was preparing global Islamic leaders. This meant training with those who were totally committed to Islam and to the implementation of *Sharia* Law throughout the world. I felt the purpose for my life was very clear. What I believed in my heart was clear, and now that needed to be expressed through my proclamation. The three aspects that needed to be addressed were a pure belief within my heart, my proclamation reflecting that belief, and my actions reflecting that proclamation.

In the teaching presented to me, anything that contradicts the laws within Islam, that being *Sharia* Law, needed to be removed. For example, when I looked at pagans, at a minimum, my heart had to consider them as pagans. Following that, if possible, I should express that with words. And ultimately, if at all possible, that should be reflected with actions. These actions would mean cleansing the community of that which is unclean, and the world desperately needed to be cleansed!

The teaching I received related to our *Jihad* continued to take me to new places of understanding. I was taught that if there was some sort of a military response from pagan Christians against Islam, we were responsible to be extra passionate to wage war, because they are actively opposing those that hold to God's laws. I was being prepared to respond to the mandate of living under *Sharia*. It was training through education, training the soul and the emotions, as well as physical and military training. This was a comprehensive package to be effective instruments in God's movement.

From 19 years of age, I was going back and forth from my sending *Madrassah* in Malaysia to my training institution in the Middle East. This continued until about the time I was 25 years old, when I was a more permanent resident of the Middle East.

At 25, I was dedicated to be a part of the global *jihad* to purify this world. Much of my new understanding of living under *Sharia* was quite foreign for the Muslim people of my home country, so I was being prepared to educate them when I returned.

Many in the Western world consider the training I undertook focused predominantly on military training so as to carry out acts of terror. But that is not the case. The focus was the embracing and implementing of a belief. It was a belief that this world was intended to live under God's law. Every aspect of the academic training I received was focused on *Sharia* Law, and the entire university body was united in their thinking on this.

Meditation was a significant part of my training. In fact, it was taught to be one of the central aspects of preparation. In meditation there were different levels of preparing our inner strength. We would always have a mentor who would guide us in our meditation and our recitation. In particular, reciting verses which referred to the supernatural support of God to our mandate; verses that were revealed to the Prophet and embraced by his followers. We would recite this with low energy, medium energy and high energy. This was all part of the preparation for the purpose of developing inner strength for when we would face challenging situations. We could expect to be alone in the implementation of our training, or we could possibly be in groups, but either way we would need this inner strength to adapt to new territories and remain strong.

We were also trained with the expectation that each of us would be self-governing and self-funding. Therefore, educational, emotional, spiritual and physical preparation did not mean that there was any institutional covering over us. It was simply preparation to be self-led. As followers of the *Sharia* Law movement, we were required to act with minimal financial dependency.

Military preparation was secondary to the preparation of the soul. However the mindset was not the mindset of secular war; it was the mindset of *Jihad,* a Holy Struggle against that which opposed God's standards, and the doing of God's will. Certainly there were secular means to fulfil this purpose, such as the use of weapons, however we had a holy purpose.

Our enemy was clear, for example if our enemy, the West, used weapons, we would respond with weapons. Anything could be used for the sake of perfecting the world under God's laws.

Within Pakistan, the Islamic university not only taught the embracing of *Sharia* Law, but created a belief and paradigm that gave the students a legitimate foundation to wage military war against Non-Muslims. The official religious training institutions, including my University, never directly carried out military training and warfare. This was beyond the eyes of any formal organisation. It was in a world where we had no structure, simply weapons with a belief that we were using them according to the will of God.

Our practice ground was Afghanistan, and this continues to be a key practice ground to this day. In Afghanistan, when I observed Soviets warring against Afghans, I saw that these people as the definition of paganism who we needed to get rid of.

I considered Pakistan and Afghanistan as near Islamic states. There was a sense of pride in a state being devoted to Islam in totality. It was like the teaching I had received in the boarding school in Malaysia could be expressed freely and totally within the new countries I now resided in. The environment here encouraged a militant attitude. This is what surprised me when I arrived in Pakistan, but at the same time encouraged me to follow Sharia law at a new level.

In my years at the Islamic boarding school in Malaysia, I had never interacted with a pagan, that being a non-Muslim. However in Pakistan and Afghanistan I observed on an increasing basis the execution of non-Muslims. It wasn't so much a shock to me, as by this stage it felt like an action that was required to be taken for God's will to take place. The jihadist actions that were being carried out in Pakistan were not something that was encouraged by most Muslims. But for us, it was the real evidence of obedience in the removal of paganism.

Chapter 4:
Bringing Sharia Law home...

In total, I spent more than 20 years preparing in the Middle East to be sent back to my country of origin. In returning, my goal wasn't to carry out acts of terror; my goal was to follow that which was I understood was perfect, God's *Sharia* Law. All methods to do this were made pure and *halal* (legal), for the purpose of living under God's law. We could raid a shop, and that was considered pure, because we were raiding that which was impure and pagan. However raids upon Muslim shops were not permitted.

All our preparation was with the expectation that we would be self-leading and self-funding. Therefore, educational, emotional, spiritual and physical preparation did not mean that there was the placing of an organisational hierarchy over us. It was simply a preparation to be able to implement an ideology that had been taught. Therefore, planning for a movement of *Sharia* Law, followers were required to act with minimal financial cost.

For nearly my entire life, whenever I read the word New Testament *(Injil)* in the *Qur'an*, my eyes did not see it, and my ears did not hear it. I knew it was considered a holy book, but if I ever saw it, it was to be burned because it was the book that was corrupted and held by pagans. The burning of the Bible was a regular practice if we came across any. Whatever unclean thing I touched or even saw, including the Bible held by the pagans, would result in me distancing myself from perfection. The actions that confronted the unclean could not be carried out in places that were clean. For example, we would not destroy a Bible in a mosque. We would not wage Holy War during the holy month of Ramadan. I didn't consider myself unclean when I destroyed that which was unclean; however, I needed to respect the sacred places of God's religion, Islam.

Life continued to be highly disciplined after I returned to my home country. I had certain responsibilities to donors who supported me. Donors were mostly from *Madrassah's*, so it was expected that I would teach and mentor students from those boarding schools. Donors provided funds, some of which was designated for operational expenses, some to cover mentoring costs, as well as funds for insurance. Despite these responsibilities, I was still governed by my belief, not the donors.

The self-governing leader of a movement needed to have a broad knowledge base of Islamic law. His followers did not necessarily have this. Often they were quite young. When someone leaves their home country, studies overseas, then returns, their influence is recognized. That was the case for me. When I returned from overseas after being trained in the implementation of *Sharia*, we were expected to be implementers of *Jihad*. That was assumed. We had no specific place we were told to go to, we simply had a belief.

Jihad is beyond the submission to worldly institutions, but involves submission to God. With *Jihad*, God is our insurance. With *Jihad*, God is the source. Our commitment to God's holy war was ultimately our own blood, and we were willing for our blood to be spilt for this purpose.

As a fighter in this Holy War, I viewed my level of holiness as greater than those around me. I had no perception that I was doing wrong. I had no concept that I was abusing basic human rights. All the actions of a person living under *Sharia* that were based upon their beliefs made their actions *halal* (legal). I was carrying out a glorious purpose, which I believed was legitimised by God. The number of people I considered to be truly carrying out God's will became smaller and smaller. The path of *Sharia* leads me to an increasingly small group of exclusivity.

Within our network, there was no room for personal relationship. We would not know our peer's family, their wife or children. We did not know each other's personal lives. But we were unified, with a common belief. Our relationships amongst fellow implementers of *Sharia* functioned differently to our relationships with the rest of the world.

When I returned to my home country and sought young people to be a part of my team, young Muslims would approach me as they viewed their joining my network as helping them personally. They didn't have a lot of *Sharia* education, but they viewed being involved in *Jihad* as beneficial for the eternal state of their souls.

In this recruitment process we could just sense in their souls and their eyes if they were one with us. We knew the people who had the same commitment as us.
I would attend the Friday prayers, and there would be possibly one or two who had that feel about them. I was very selective, as they were to be part of a pioneering movement.

When someone falls in love, there's an emotional connection. When people have the same spirit as I had, there was an emotional connection. So those who were a part of our network were those who had a passion. They were passionate to come to me, rather than the emphasis being on me to recruit them. In the recruitment of members, it was not even their commitment to the pillars of Islam, such as their commitment to *sholat,* to fast, or their commitment to give. It was beyond this. It was an emotional tie.

Our objective was that my home nation would be totally committed to *Sharia.* Certainly a key part of this was the education of young people in dozens of *Madrassah's* in my home country. The foundational teachings concerning *Sharia* Law within many of these *Madrassah's* was already present, but their commitment to the application of it was lacking. I was declaring to them that this was the moment for our nation to live under God's law. Generally, there was fertile soil in regards to the acceptance of *Sharia* Law.

However, awareness of my activities increasingly developed in the government, as I became more active and extreme in my pursuit of *Sharia* Law.

My parents became embarrassed and ashamed in front of their community, as their son grew to be an instrument of terror and a regular story in the media. I was outworking a very different type of Islam to that which their community understood and practised.

Part 2:

My Foundations Are Shaken

A journey from extremism to love

Chapter 5:
Inner turmoil begins!

When I returned to my home country, my dream was that within a short space of time people would change to live under *Sharia* Law. In fact, the goal for the network of committed people was that within 12 years my nation would be transformed to live under God's rule. This was despite the government opposing the implementation of *Sharia*.

Our movement was feared by common Muslims. Our view was that the Islam practiced within this country was tolerant of paganism, and this was incompatible with a country living under God's laws. Our goal as Muslims was to have a country that lived under the perfect law, a country that was clean. And so, we needed to carry out *Jihad* with our whole being. We established *Madrassahs* to be a base from which to see this mandate fulfilled. We were very optimistic, because God was with us in our holy struggle.

When our government changed, we had increased opportunity as the new powers gave us greater credibility. This was in contrast to the previous government, who viewed our institutions as illegitimate.

My fellow peers were strong in carrying out the purification of areas that suffered a pagan presence. Areas that previously lived in harmony now lived in chaos, as we endeavoured to create communities that would live under God's Holy Law. Because I was prepared more with an academic education for a holy struggle, my own role did not usually involve the sort of physical actions my peers implemented. But the passion to wage war was common to us all. The passion to purify any unclean areas was within us all. These activities were not coordinated under a central command. There were numerous groups, and our authority was from God.

However, the irony of this situation was that my soul was in turmoil. During this time, I began to experience depression and began to doubt our mandate. There were many challenges and obstacles. There were numerous failures in opposing the pagan centres. There were many mistakes in implementing our mandate. An attempt to bomb a church totally failed, and instead of destroying the church itself, it was only things outside of the church premises that were damaged. I began to be, in my own eyes, a failure in this holy struggle.

The failed bombing was a hit to my self-belief. I became increasingly depressed. I thought, "All this preparation and education, and I'm not even close to achieving what I had attempted to pursue."

Besides this, an ongoing sense of hypocrisy nagged from within. On the outside I was the model for Islamic standards, however within I felt a failure. The core belief regarding our struggle against paganism was deeply a part of me, but I was becoming emotionally tired regarding the implementation of *Sharia*. I began to question myself.

After 20 years of preparation, I felt I should be achieving more. At the same time, I saw many peers who seemed to be highly productive. For some reason, it was different for them. My heart still believed in the education I received, my mouth recited the verses I learnt, but my actions couldn't reflect my heart and my words. I was simply disappointed with myself. Depression created within me weakness to act, and the weakness to act created increasing depression.

I became unable to implement the purification of communities with physical action. My passion and energy was lame and crippled. The hatred towards the West was still there, but I was helpless in my hatred. I could only pour out my heart to myself. There was no concept of personal transparency with fellow warriors of *Jihad*. I was extremely lonely. I couldn't express my heart to anyone, especially not to people who were disobedient in following the *Sharia* Law.

The whole system I lived in created loneliness. I could not truly interact with others. My relationship with my wife could not help me in this trauma. According to *Sharia* Law she was on a different level to me as a woman, and there was to be no personal sharing with her. My life was filled with hundreds - even thousands - of people. I was a leader to many *Madrassah's*. But I was all alone.

My mind was in such turmoil at this time. Later, when I realised that all my peers experienced this turmoil as well, I knew I was living life under a curse.

When Cain spilt the blood of his brother Abel, Cain didn't want to know about his brother's blood. But the blood of Abel still cried out to God. So God responded to the call of that blood said to Cain, "Where is your brother?" "Am I my brother's keeper?" Cain replied. God said, "The blood of Abel has cried out to me." And then because of that crying out, God calls out, "Cursed are you."

With the curse upon the one who spilt blood, the cursed one wanted to run. But God said to Cain and his type,

> "*People will want to kill you, but they will not be able to.*"
> *(Genesis 4:15)*

That is the trauma of one who spills blood. The cursed life, the fearful life, is transferred to the followers of Cain. I believe that when anyone came to Cain, he wanted to kill because of the crying out of blood within his mind and soul.

This was the reality of my life. When I tried to sleep, I couldn't, because there began to be a whisper in my ear:
"You are cursed."
"You are a murderer."
I had acted with no value for blood or life. I was cursed and I could only transfer that curse upon others. It was like my peers and I

needed the blood of others to sustain our own life, but for me personally, my life was no longer being sustained by this.

I am sharing this analogy in hindsight. At the time I wouldn't have referred to myself as cursed, but my response certainly reflected the response of Cain. On the surface I viewed myself as doing no wrong; on the contrary, I was doing God's will. But ultimately, my soul was responding because of a curse. This curse was the cry of the innocent.

Like the story of Cain and Abel, the ground where blood has been spilt is cursed. Afghanistan lives under this curse. How many cases of spilt blood have there been in this nation? The blood continues to cry out. And the person who caused the blood to be spilt lives under a curse wherever he goes. The heart of a man that is cursed will seek more spilt blood. This is terrifying. There is a need to be free from this cycle.

For example, in the past when there was *Jihad* to liberate our brothers in Afghanistan from the pagans, there was extensive spilling of blood. But the ground remained cursed once the 'pagans' left, even to this day. The land of Afghanistan is not a land that is blessed, but is cursed, because of the cry of the blood.

Whether for the country of Afghanistan, or for individuals like myself, there needs to be a breaking of the curse. The fact that every day there is a desire to see more blood spilt, is evidence that there is a continued living under a curse. The heart is in turmoil and the mind is in turmoil when the soul is under a curse. From generation to generation, the story of Cain and Abel continues.

Chapter 6:
Meeting my enemy

In the context I lived in, nearly everyone was my enemy. I would never sit down and have a friendly conversation with my Muslim family or friends, let alone a pagan! In this dark life where I was living in loneliness, I was seeking through supernatural ways a solution to my trauma. I was asking for a solution from God, according to my belief system. I was layered in loneliness, which I kept concealed from others.

In this time of loneliness, I met with a young man called Farid. It was a unique meeting with a Muslim who seemed to be very different to most.

The timing of the meeting with this Islamic educator was unplanned, however as I was seeking for a solution for my personal problems, I saw in him something that my soul longed for. I saw he had an inner strength that I needed.

I couldn't manipulate Farid to become one of my followers. It seemed his strength was greater than mine. I was careful not to give him the impression he was my teacher, as I was the one who was the 'expert of the Law'. Nevertheless we began to meet regularly. I started to realise he had more influence on me than I on him. Until that point, I had always been the more influential, more powerful one with anyone I had interacted with, and brought them on my journey rather than being pulled into theirs.

It was as if the foundations for my beliefs were increasingly becoming inadequate the more I met with him. We prayed together during Friday prayers. We visited my *Madrassah's*; we talked in the mosque, studying the *Qur'an* together. He was very different to the other Islamic educators I knew and we were exchanging beliefs and understanding.

The criterion for gauging the commitment of a Muslim generally is the fluency of their *sholat* (prayer). So I thought Farid was perhaps quite new to Islam. This Islamic educator was not exact in following Islamic tradition. In addition to this, he frequently discussed the person of Jesus, and referred to the Bible as still being relevant as a pillar of faith for Muslims.

Farid's interpretation and understanding of the *Qur'an* was beyond mine in many ways. I had expertise in recitation and in the implementation of *Sharia* Law. This man pursued understanding by examining the context of each verse of the *Qur'an*, with minimal attention to following Islamic tradition. Despite Farid's shortcomings, his teaching about Islam was very inspiring, and this process of dialogue between us continued for years.

Then the moment came when he explained he was a disciple of Jesus. I exploded in rage. I explained to him that I believed in Jesus, but certainly not as my master!

However as I continued to meet with Farid, I was drawn to something in his message. I felt conflicted about the close bond I had with him. On one hand, I hated him so much, but on the other, Farid was the only friend I had.

It was at this stage that another dramatic event occurred. I was being accused by the authorities of an act of terror! This, I thought, was surely the end of my life. Crimes of this nature were typically punished by execution. But I wasn't ready for it; I was filled with fear and had no-one to turn to.

My friend, this disciple of Jesus, began to share with me about the state of man's sinful heart and the solution of a holy sacrifice. When Farid spoke about this, he spoke of the lame and the sick 2000 years ago being given a solution to their life's trauma. He spoke of Jesus being enabled by God to bring a solution to life's greatest problem. He said just like the lame 2000 years ago, I could also find a solution to my greatest need.

This was all in accordance with the *Qur'an*, which I had embraced. Farid was showing me this figure of Jesus within the *Qur'an* and how He was able to provide a solution. I was in desperate need, just like those people 2000 years ago. He explained that despite the serious accusation I faced, Jesus had authority to bring a solution.

My friend Farid told me to pray to God in the name of Jesus. He told me that Jesus has authority to help mankind's problems, even my impossible situation, if I would believe in Him.

I felt unimaginable emotional agony and conflict to even mention that name of Jesus. I was going against everything I had been taught since I was a child. Just the thought of calling out in that name made me physically sick. But I had no other solution to the greatest challenge of my life, and execution was awaiting me. I called repeatedly to my friend and asked for him to pray on my behalf. Farid said he couldn't! The words needed to come from my mouth.

In this state of helplessness, I had nowhere to run and nothing to turn to, except to follow the suggestion of this person.

My willingness to suffer for *Sharia* became non-existent. Any previous inner strength I had was brought to null. I now just held onto a prayer, this wild hope for a solution. I couldn't do anything else. It was a 5 second prayer crying for help, and that's when a miracle happened.

Suddenly a number of confessions came forward from within the *Sharia* network. The punishment I was facing was for a series of deadly bombings; however those people who were really behind the attacks came forward. Charges against me were dropped. My prayer and the glimmer of hope I had held to was miraculously answered.

I was going to be executed, I am now free. I was going to be declared guilty, I am now declared innocent.

I began to understand the unclean state of my human heart. Each time I met with my friend I was strongly encouraged to meditate on and pray about what he told me. I believed in the prophet Jesus previously - but to have faith in His words and receive Jesus, this was something I had no understanding of. I finally came to a point of recognising His authority and having a new spirit within my heart. I knew that receiving Jesus was not a result of my obedience to following God's law.

There was a powerful change within me, which was transforming the state of my heart. This began to affect my words and my actions. When my heart was changed by God's Spirit, it was totally different from trying to change through my own self-initiative. There was a miracle that happened inside. I didn't confess a lot of words, I didn't say a lot of things, there was just a miracle happening inside as God Himself worked within me.

The foundations and structure of my previous belief system began to change. The explanation of the person mentoring me was that he did not want to take the position of the teacher, or spiritual leader. This was the task of God Himself.

It was like I walked out of a dark room, layered with darkness, and entered one filled with light. When this change of heart took place, many people started asking what happened to me. In particular, my own wife and children saw a dramatic change in my appearance and demeanour. However psychologically, I was still carrying the effects of my past actions, and I noticed this particularly as I began to meet some Westerners. Meeting Asian Christians was not such a psychological challenge for me, however I was certainly aware of these mental scars whenever I met Western Christians.

I found the experience of meeting Western Christians traumatic for years to come. My Islamic educator friend seemed to have a number of these Western friends, so I had to deal with this experience regularly.

One time in my role as an *Imam*[9] (which I continue to this day) I spoke to a group of Asian Christians. Afterwards, I was invited to one of these Christians' house for lunch, and an American climbed in the car to drive. That was the first time in my new life I had come so close to a Western Christian. The wounds were still open and my mind was racing, but that was the beginning of a peace within my soul and the changing of my attitude towards the West. In fact, in future years as an Imam, I would embrace this Western man as part of my spiritual family.

I was becoming free.

A Western Christian speaks of his meeting with Usman Kadir:

At one point in time, a group of Islamic leaders, Ismail Yasin, Farid Ibrahim and Usman Kadir, held a two-day meeting for Christians to attend and learn more about the Islamic faith. These Islamic Leaders realised that Christians viewed the original message of Islam as being based upon modern *Jihad*. These men viewed Islam very differently, and desired to share this understanding.

At the end of the meeting, my wife who attended invited all of them to come over to our house. I went to the location to pick them up and Usman got into the car very slowly. Other than that, I didn't notice anything unusual about him as he was in back seat. However I found out later that he was extremely scared and shocked to be in the car with me, a Western Christian; he thought this was a conspiracy and someone was out to get him. Usman guessed that someone had found out about his past, and had therefore arranged for him to travel in my car.

---

[9] *An Imam is the religious leader within the mosque leading the Islamic prayer.*

When we got to our house, I went inside and Usman waited out in the front yard. He slowly began to move towards the house as I waited, holding the front door open for him. On the front verandah he fell to his knees. Ismail and Farid thought he had fallen over and they helped him up, bringing him into the lounge room. By this time he was crying uncontrollably. Usman's face was on the floor, he was holding my ankles, loudly sobbing.

I didn't feel it was anything demonic, and although the situation was strange, there was a strong sense of peace in the room. After about ten minutes of crying at my feet, Usman started asking, "Can you forgive me? Can you forgive me?" I had no idea what he was talking about. I had never met him in my life! I reached down to put my hand on his shoulder. His head was still on my ankles, and my feet were completely wet with his tears. I just said, "I forgive you." My hand was on his back while he was shaking and sobbing. I said again, "I forgive you, I forgive you," without even knowing what his anguish was about.

After some time we helped Usman up on a chair, but by this stage he was so weak from crying he could hardly sit. Once he was on the chair he began to tell his story, but he would only get through one or two sentences before spending many more minutes sobbing.

He would say, "I was a part of killing many Westerners," and then he would begin sobbing once more. He would fall back on the floor, grabbing my ankles again, asking, "Can you forgive me? Can you forgive me?" I would tell him again, "Yes I forgive you. God forgives you." Then he would be down another five or ten minutes sobbing, followed by us helping him back up on the chair again. Then another sentence; "I have been responsible for torturing Western Christians. Can you forgive me?" He would fall on the floor and cry for another ten minutes. It was a long time that this pattern continued, perhaps up to two hours.

A lot of this repentance was related to being associated with acts of terror against the Soviets in Afghanistan. By the end of the two hours, Usman was completely exhausted and we had to lay him on a bed, where he rested and then reappeared later on in the day. Ismail and Farid explained the background to some of Usman's life. They explained how since he had come back from life in the Middle East, he had tried to implement *Sharia* in the country in which I reside, however in recent years there had been a transformation in Usman's life and he had accepted Jesus as his master.

That day was the first time Usman had ever met a white Western man at such proximity. His work since his return from the Middle East was based solely in Islamic boarding schools. I was the first Western male he had ever talked to, and all of his memories of the past were flashing through his mind when he saw me.

I am sure it was an amazing work of healing in his life that day. I am grateful that I could be a part of that process. Pak Usman expressed his deep-seated hatred for the West, in particular Western men, whom he had a vengeful hatred towards. It was at least an hour before he could look at me in the eyes, by which time his eyes were all red and swollen with tears. But by the end of the day we were hugging and laughing. I explained how God wants to bring restoration and healing to his life from these things.

Chapter 7:
Sin and solution

Following my cry to God for a solution, my world was being shaken and turned upside down. God revealed to me a moment that blood was spilt on this earth, where instead of calling out and resulting in a curse upon me as an evildoer, it called out to God for my forgiveness.

Despite my long journey of over 30 years in seeking a sacrifice that is pleasing to God through *Jihad*, I give thanks that there has been a change in my heart and recognition that God has provided the solution.

The solution that He has provided has redeemed the separation between God and man. The sole figure that fulfilled the requirement for holy blood was Jesus. His holiness guarantees a solution to sin, and with this, my personal turmoil has been finished.

The vital thing I needed to consider is the way that sin is viewed in the eyes of God. Since Adam and Eve, God views all mankind as living in sin. Because of this, Adam hid himself in the garden, away from God. Since that moment, mankind has continually endeavoured to see how he can reach the standards required of God. This endeavour defined my life for decades as I pursued *Sharia* Law. It is now clear to me that mankind is not able of its own accord to reach the standard of holiness required to experience the presence of God.

The interesting thing is that sin is related to our blood. Within our traditions of Islam, at least according to those who embrace *Sharia* Law, the ultimate endeavour to restore our standing before God is to allow our own personal blood to be poured out for His sake.

In one of the major celebrations of Islam, *Idul Adha*, which celebrates Abraham's obedience, there is a sacrifice of blood. But an animal sacrifice remains unacceptable to bridge the divide between God and man. Why is this so? Because the sins of man demanded the sacrifice of a man, a great sacrifice.

In the attitude of a Muslim carrying out *Jihad*, he views himself as a candidate of martyrdom, whether that view is correct or not. The point I'm making here is that the solution to sin is intrinsically connected with blood.

The question is, is the blood of the *Jihad* Martyr *halal* (pure and holy)? The view of a *jihadist* is that his blood is *halal*, however, it is clear that this is a mistaken view in the eyes of God. For example, when our ancestors fell into sin, the attitude of mankind was to pursue a solution. The first solution was to find a leaf as a covering. However that leaf did not contain any element of blood. Therefore, God rejected that solution of man. God said He would provide them clothing from the skins of animals. This means that God shed the blood of animals to clothe them in the garden.

Secondly, we continue with the story of Cain and Abel. One pursued a blood sacrifice; the other pursued a sacrifice from the grains of the earth, a non-blood sacrifice. That which was accepted contained the element of blood, and that which did not contain the element of blood was rejected. Sin and its solution are inherently tied to blood.

Within Islam, this is a truth that is woven throughout our traditions. However tragically, the blood that is committed to God is not holy and pure in His eyes. It is not the blood that is prepared and planned by God. Islam is crying for holy blood.

God needs a pure sacrifice. Only He can provide that. Not me, not a martyr, and not a lamb. If we were to be the ones to provide the solution, Abraham would have certainly continued in the action of sacrificing his son. But, God intervened with Abraham, because even his son's blood was not pure to enable reconciliation. We can see throughout Scripture that it is only God who can provide the pure and holy sacrifice that is needed.

The following verses from the *Qur'an* also explain this:

> *When they (Abraham and his son) had both surrendered, and he lay him face down, we[10] called "Abraham", you have fulfilled the vision. We reward those who do good. This was a clear test. And we ransomed him with a great sacrifice. (QS 36: 102 – 107)[11]*

Muslims understand from this verse *"That God ransomed Abraham's child with a great sacrifice."* Muslims today believe that Ishmael was the child on Mount Moriah. Christians believe Isaac was the child on Mount Moriah. That is a non-issue, because whether Isaac or Ishmael, God ransomed *all* with a great sacrifice.

The problem is, we have never been told what that great sacrifice is. It was the sacrifice of the Holy One. It was a man paying the price for a man. When we read the story of God's provision of a solution for sin, in providing the perfect man, according to Islam, and the *Qur'an*, there is only one without sin. That is Jesus.

> *The Angel said (to Mary), "I am truly a messenger of your Lord to give you a sinless boy." (QS 19:19)*

---

[10] *Within the Qur'an, as with other Semitic languages, "We" is used for when God is speaking to represent God's majesty, as well as to indicate the involvement of Angels in God's interaction with mankind.*

[11] *Within this book there are a number of quotes from the Qur'an. It is helpful for the reader to remember that the Qur'an is in poetic Arabic from the East in the 7th century. Translations in modern English will be somewhat limited in its ability to communicate.*

With this sinless sacrifice, the blood of reconciliation was received by the God of Abraham. Without a realisation of this truth, continued efforts of sacrifice, even martyrdom by Islamic brothers, will continue to take place as the search goes on to find blood that is acceptable to God.

When we understand truth and when we are guided by God, we will understand that God has provided the blood sacrifice. And that holy sacrifice, Jesus, spoke out and said, "It is finished!" When we accept this our hearts are filled with peace because there has been a true solution for sin. For me, this is the most glorious thing; that Jesus said, "IT IS FINISHED!" (John 19:30) These are the most beautiful words for me.

Previously I was an extremist in my religion. An extremist has many problems. My own name is now plastered over the internet because of my problems, and the problems I caused. I should be dead because of what I have been through, but today I am writing to you because Jesus said, "It is finished".

I am here because there is someone who has finished my problems with God. He does not hold those problems against me anymore. I am still a leader of faith, and I want to help many people overcome their difficulties. I tell them to repent and have faith; to believe in the one who said, "It is finished".

I previously believed as a leader of *Sharia* Law, that for God, I was His instrument of *Jihad*. The final solution was to die and try to take many others with me. There was no light and my problems increased. I lived in darkness!

In that darkness I was pushed to know Jesus. I gave Him my darkness. I heard the words, "It is finished", and because of those words I can write to you today. In the natural I cannot write to you, but with God, the impossible becomes possible.

Naturally, I still look at myself and remember the terror I caused, asking myself, "Am I rubbish?" But no, I am created by God, and remember His words that as for my life of terror, "IT IS FINISHED!"

Seeing the World
Through New Eyes

A journey from extremism to love

Chapter 8:
Seeing the world with new eyes

I'd like to share some of the most important areas of my thinking and understanding which have been completely transformed since giving my life to Jesus. These include my understanding of Islam, of *Sharia* and *Jihad*, but also my understanding of Jesus, of Christians, and of key relationships in my life – such as my relationship with my wife. God has brought transformation to each of these areas.

Seeing Muhammad through new eyes

During the months following my acceptance of Jesus, I would sit with my friend, Farid, and together read the *Qur'an* and the Bible in a new way. My studies no longer focused upon Arabic recitation. It was no longer centred on *Sharia* Law. It was as if we gave ourselves permission to pursue truth together. Truth was like someone alive within us, and we excitedly followed wherever truth would lead us.

With the benefit of Farid's studies, I began to reconstruct my understanding of the *Qur'an*. I would attempt to understand the context of each verse from the *Qur'an*, and the chronology of each event in our pursuit of understanding the Messenger of Islam. It was at this time that a realisation became clearer to me. I cried out as I understood the implications - I had spent my entire life directly opposing the mission of the Prophet Muhammad!

I had spent my life training people to oppose the Bible and the people who held to its teaching. I now saw that Muhammad spent his life introducing the Bible to Arabia! I had spent my life circulating hatred towards the name of Jesus. Muhammad introduced Him to Arabia as the Word from God, the most glorious one.

The Bible and the prophets of the Bible are the pillars of the Islamic faith introduced by Muhammad to Arabia. Throughout my life in implementing modern *Sharia*, I was an *enemy* of the mission of my Prophet.

Allow me to explain further.

The prophet Muhammad had a close and intimate connection with the God of Abraham, Isaac and Jacob. His understanding drew him close to the people of the Book, to the Christians. Why do I say this? Muhammad himself was an Arab, and according to Islamic tradition he was a descendant of Ishmael. When he proclaimed Islam, he proclaimed a message which did not contain his own Arab origins. Because of this, he became an enemy of his own race, the *Quraysh*[12] of Mecca.

His message did not make the Arab people the central figures in this belief system. For example, the God that he was calling his own Arab people to worship was the God of Abraham, Isaac and Jacob. It was not the gods of the local Arab traders. Concerning the faith that he was calling his Arab peoples to embrace, it had strong ties with the faith of Christians. Concerning the Holy books, remembering that the Arabic *Qur'an* did not exist in the time of Muhammad, he was calling his Arab people to a revealed truth contained in the Scriptures that were held by Christians.

Muhammad suffered because he refused to embrace much of the Arab belief system and tradition. So, now we ask the question, what was the view of Muhammad towards Christians? It may well have been a more intimate relationship than with his own people!

Today in modern Islam, all this has changed! There is a massive chasm between Christianity and Islam. And the Islam that is

---

[12] *The ruling tribe of Mecca at the time of the birth of the Prophet Muhammad*

being presented to the nations of the world is predominantly focused upon Arab culture.

In this sense, modern Islam often opposes the mission of Muhammad. Modern Islam is presenting that the true Holy Book is from Arabia, the true Prophet is from Arabia, and the true Holy City is from Arabia. This is the exact opposite of the mission of Muhammad. The result of this is in modern Islam is that both the message of Christians and close relationships with Christians is foreign. Even *Sharia* Law originally reflected not Arab law, but Hebrew law (although *Sharia* Law related to a local kingdom context of Medina, See chapter 10). The 25 prophets of Islam are Hebrew prophets. We cannot lie about the realities of history. Modern Islam has departed from the mission of Muhammad!

When Muhammad received his first revelations concerning the one true God, he went together with his godly wife, Siti Khadijah, directly to a Christian by the name of Waraqa Ibn Nawfal. (See Appendix 2 for an analysis on this key individual in Muhammad's life) Waraqa Ibn Nawfal was someone who was translating the New Testament from Hebrew into Arabic. This was the person who the prophet Muhammad sought confirmation as to whether his departure from the idolatry of Mecca to the surrender to the God of Abraham was truth. So we see that the first person to hear the messenger of Islam's revelation was a Christian.

How could we have moved so far from the origins of Islam? How could someone who suffered as a result of introducing the Old and New Testament as the true Holy Books to Arabia be so misrepresented?

I cannot undo the years that have past me by. However I can be a voice for my people for the future. I can follow the message of the Messenger of Islam. That is, to bring the Bible (Torah, Zabur and Injil) back to the Islamic people, the Bible being a pillar of Islam as presented by the Prophet to Arabia.

Seeing Jihad with new eyes

Jihad is a very controversial and emotional topic within Islam itself, let alone outside of Islam. *Jihad* always presents a negative stigma to non-Muslims. With this I need to explain the origin and meaning of the word *Jihad*. It is a word that was used in many aspects of life, prior to Islam, to refer to a struggle. Every struggle, whether that be economic, political, religious, or even day-to-day mundane struggles, were referred to as a *jihad*. *Jihad* was not necessarily a religious word. If I get up in the morning and struggle to get my hair in the right place, that is my personal *jihad*!

Over time, this term was applied to the monotheist and the pain they experienced in the beginning days of Islam. In its original meaning and use, the word *Jihad* had many parallels with the word Islam. Examining its etymology, the word Islam means to surrender in totality to the Hebrew God. The word Islam is an active word of surrendering one's self to the one True God. The process of this was *jihad*, the struggle within one's self to come to a place of surrender.

The outworking of Islam was therefore closely connected to the meaning of *Jihad*. For example, in Islam, when there was surrender to the God of Abraham, there were blessings for obedience to God's commands and there was punishment for disobedience. The outworking of this requires energy, and that energy is our *jihad*. Therefore someone carries out *jihad* to implement the commands that have come from God, and oppose and reject the actions that are disobedient to God. When Jesus says in his ultimate, greatest command to do all that he commanded, and to make disciples of all peoples, this reflects very well the definition and nature of the word *jihad*.

If God tells you to do something and you don't do it, that's evidence of a lack of *jihad*. A community that carries out *jihad* according to its true meaning lives a godly life that reflects the commands from God.

There is a temptation to be arrogant and to consider all those who are not carrying out spiritual *jihad* to be of lesser value than you. In its origin however, jihad required humility. You cannot be surrendered and be arrogant! *Jihad* and Islam should affect how you view others if you are someone who is truly surrendered. However, this was not case with me, as I used to view my peers and I as the ultimate example of godly living and others as lowly. This contradicts the definition of Islam.

It is this attitude of *jihad* that has corrupted Islam. There is an understanding from the beginning that those who do not surrender, those who are not Islam, are not a part of God's people. When I use Islam in this context, I am not referring to an institutional allegiance. I am using it in its original and generic sense of surrender, whether in regards to those who are Muslim, Christian or Jewish. This is consistent with all the scriptures. Our *jihad* towards those who have not surrendered to the God of Abraham begins with our heart, and then our words. But the *jihad* that is known today is only a physical *jihad*.

In the 7th century, *jihad* included a physical threat to the pagans of Arabia if they did not leave their idolatry and turn to God, but it was a form of *jihad* that was culturally more appropriate in the era of Mohammad, the culture of nomadic raids. (See chapter 10) The *jihad* of Muhammad had the goal of uniting the warring tribes in Arabia. Muhammad's *jihad* was to have them leave paganism and lead them to monotheism. His *jihad* was to implement social reform.

Now I see my world with new eyes. That was the culture and context of 7th century Arabia, but God is merciful and compassionate, and the *jihad* that we carry out should be a heart surrendered to God, that with an attitude of humility, that also directs others to the merciful and compassionate God. This is our *jihad*.

When I look at my world with new eyes in regard to *Jihad*, I realize that Arab tribes lived in paganism previously, and that *Jihad* was not just a spiritual act in that context, but a political act in unifying Arab tribes. Some of the revelation that Mohammad received is in this context. My *jihad* now is my energy to live my life according to God's will and being obedient to the commands of God that were revealed through Jesus.

Previously, I would have supported the physical *jihad* against those who did not act according to God's laws, the *Sharia,* and certainly given support to *jihad* against those outside of Islam. They were considered to be of lesser human value than those within Islam.

Now, with new eyes I see that even though there are those who act in opposition to God's standards, it is only God who can carry out judgment. That right to carry out judgment has been designated to the only Holy One, Jesus himself.

An accepting and embracing of the message of Jesus brings us back to the original meaning of *jihad*. We leave the distorted view of many today, and embrace a true *jihad*; that of living our lives according to the commands of the Holy One from God.

Seeing Sharia Law through new eyes

Sharia Law's birthplace was in the city of Medina. There were certainly cases of commands in Medina to kill Christians. However we need to understand that this was in the context of local kingdom law according to the kingdom of Medina's constitution. We also need to understand that the context of Medina, being set a town within the Arabian Desert in the 7th century, is a very different context to the world we live in of the 21st century.

For Muslims today, *Sharia* is a law that came from God for the purpose of enabling man to live according to God's perfect standards. The task of man is to live out the things that are commanded by God and to reject the things which are forbidden by God on planet earth. This is the *Sharia* of God. The *Sharia* is for those who have surrendered themselves to God and who recognize God as the ultimate guide and instructor for living life on earth.

The question is, does God implement *Sharia*, or man? In my former life I believed that mankind, specifically I, was to be the instrument of imposing God's standards upon mankind. The fruit of this was full of negative results. It was full of destruction. It was full of hatred.

Today in this world, those carrying out of *Sharia* do not understand the issue of whether it is man or God who should implement this. Man is trying to organise and place God on the face of the earth. Man is imposing God's standards and holiness by force. All of this is done through man's hand and not God's. So that we can avoid this disaster, avoid this destruction, and avoid the desire to spill blood, we need to stop putting ourselves in the place of God.

We need to look with new eyes at God's standards. He is our guide, not man, to live by His righteous standards. It is His Spirit who leads us away from the path of destruction. Only God can do that. So today I look with new eyes, looking to God, not man. Man brings destruction, whereas God restores. I see the traditional understanding of *Sharia* as man taking the place of God. However God's judgments are unfathomable; man can never take this place.

To further explore the meaning of *Sharia*, I would like to talk about the role of the Holy Spirit. The understanding within Islam is that the Holy Spirit is the Spirit from God. There is a slight difference between this and the understanding of the Holy Spirit in traditional Christianity. Today Islam rarely explores the topic of the Spirit of God - it is not appropriate to be discussed. However, in the early days of Islam, this was not the case. The prophet Muhammad often revealed and discussed the Spirit of God. When the messenger of Islam was asked, "where did you get this revelation?" He explained that the Spirit of God revealed it to him.

The *Sharia* of God should be implemented and directed by the Spirit of God, not by man. Therefore, mankind's heart will be prepared as a holy dwelling place for God. When I was the implementer of *Sharia*, my heart could not be a dwelling place for the Spirit – it was contaminated. We are not able to purify ourselves, only God can purify our hearts.

The Holy Spirit as implementer of *Sharia* will result in us loving our neighbour as we love ourselves. The guidance of the Spirit of God results in love. The guidance under the control of *Sharia* from man results in intimidation. This is the contrast of living by the Spirit of God, as opposed to living under man as the implementer of *Sharia*.

The standards that were set for the political state of Medina by the messenger of Islam were given in a very different context to what exists today. For example, Muslims at the time of Muhammad were not to associate themselves and their camp with pagans. Who were the pagans, according to Muhammad, in that era? The pagans were the *Quraysh* Arabs of Mecca, Muhammad's own ethnic group, not Jews and Christians. These people were worshipers of idols in the *Kaaba*[13]. So the pagans in the era of the birth of Islam were actually Arabs!

Amongst the Christians and Jews, there were those who Muhammad considered as worshipers of the God of Abraham. These were considered by him to be Islam, i.e. those who were

---

[13] *A square stone building in the centre of the Great Mosque at Mecca*

submitted to God. And then there were those who Muhammad viewed as idolaters, based upon their actions. This included Jews who rejected Jesus as Messiah. However ultimately, any effort to transplant the local laws of an ancient kingdom into another era and another context and force that upon people as God's laws will only end in destruction.

Personally, my view concerning *Sharia* is that it is religious law designed for a physical and local context in 7th Century Arabia. The essence of this law is the carrying of external religious forms that does not deal with the issues of the heart. Jesus revealed the heart of man required something far beyond this.

Seeing my wife with new eyes

I met my wife-to-be for the first time in 1995 in an Islamic boarding school, one year after returning to my home country. It was a unique meeting, because she was from one of the boarding schools that I oversaw, and she was one of the students who was educated by me. Towards the end of her education, I got to know her parents and family, and that was the beginning of an increasingly closer relationship with my future wife.

During that time and during the start of my marriage to her, I was very active in promoting Sharia law in my home country. When I had a dramatic change in my life, and in particular, when I began to read the Bible, it was quite a challenge for my wife initially.

When my wife was feeling the pain of me facing execution, she was observing and realising the process I was going through, including seeing Farid direct me to the figure that could provide a solution for my problem. She could see the evidence personally, that a solution was provided when I cried out to God in Jesus' name in my crisis. At this time, my children were very young, only

3 or 4 years old, and they had no knowledge of the challenge their father was facing. But I am sure the change in my character was evident for them also, including how I spoke to them.

There was no denying for my wife that she preferred her transformed husband than the husband whom she married. Today my household, including my twin boys, all share a common belief in Christ.

According to *Sharia* law, obedience to God is to be implemented by the whole household. If it is not, it counted as disobedience on the part of the husband, the head. The husband was responsible for the godly actions of his household from the time that the household woke from sleep, until that evening when they went to bed. This was a major change in practice for the federation of the Arab tribes, as previously, many of the tribes followed a matrimonial system.

In my old way of seeing the world, I was very extreme in this interpretation. I considered my wife to be of lesser value than me and beneath me in status. This was how I understood women's purpose as created by God. The function and status of women was lower to serve the sexual needs and other daily needs of a man. I also believed this status continued into the afterlife.

Before I experienced transformation within my heart, everything within our household was organised by my command, as the head. However, now I realise that my wife brings completeness to me; she is my helper. I realised that if someone is a helper, then they have a value that I do not have. My paradigm changed.

I now view my wife as my helper, as one who brings completeness and a woman of great value to walk alongside of me.

Our world cannot continue to exist without women. Regeneration cannot continue except for the value of the woman. My children go to my wife for tenderness. They certainly didn't see that in me when I was living under *Sharia!*

With a transformed heart and new eyes to see the world, I realised that God created man for one woman only. When my wife realised this change in my thinking, she was full of joy! Jesus said,

> *"In Heaven there will not be marriage."* We all have our favourite verses within Scripture. My wife's favourite verse is when Jesus said her husband would not have 70 virgins in heaven!
> *(Matt 22:30)*

When she also accepted the Old and New Testament as truth, my wife's view of how God viewed women changed. When Muslim women hear the true value that God places upon them, they will jump up and down and dance!

During the Age of Ignorance (*Jahiliyyah*[14]) in pre-Islam Arabia, women often had the status close to that of non-human. Female babies were often buried alive, because their presence in this world was considered unclean. The role of females was almost equivalent to objects that simply fulfilled the lust of the flesh.

Sadly, some of Islam today has returned to *Jahiliyyah*, the age of ignorance, where women are of a non-human status. I believe this is a false understanding of what is presented in the *Qur'an*. In fact, Scriptures show the incredible value and worth that God places on women. I now see my world with new eyes, and know that I'm not complete without my wife.

I'd like to add a quick note on the rest of my family life here. After many years of being separated from my parents, I had a brief opportunity to meet with my father in his final months before he passed away. My parents had known me as someone who had embraced extreme views of Islam. Although they were devout in their practice of Islamic

---

[14] The Islamic Age of Spiritual Ignorance, primarily referring to Arabia prior to Muhammad

traditions, they were embarrassed to see me follow what they viewed as extremist ideas. However, in this final parting before my father passed away, he saw a new man. It was a brief time, where they welcomed me back and welcomed the change that had occurred within me.

Seeing Christians with new eyes

Growing up, the term Christian was simply a word that contained negative connotations. The *Qur'an* mentions negative issues with Christians in specific contexts. However these issues that occurred in Muhammad's era have now been transplanted to Islam today. Within the *Jihad* I carried out, it was these ancient issues that I was carrying within me.

Before I had a changed heart, I saw Christians as those who practiced paganism. There was no sense of closeness. What's more, I didn't recognise they carried the spiritual truth coming from a common father, which is Abraham. Life was full of suspicion towards the motivation of Christians, especially when they carried out humanitarian activity towards the Islamic community.

However, when we look at the Islamic Holy Book as a whole, we realise that there should be closeness and a bond between one another.

> *And nearest among them in love to the believers will you find those who say, 'We are Christians,' because amongst these are men devoted to learning and men who have renounced the world, and they are not arrogant"*
> *(QS 5:82)*

If I honestly speak about the proclamation of the messenger of Islam, it leaves me with no choice but to acknowledge that we are of a common family. The beginning actions of Muhammad were immediately connected with and confirmed by a Christian minister, that being Waraqa bin Naufal. In contrast to this, the pagan tribes of Mecca that were living in spiritual darkness represented those that opposed Muhammad.

Islamic tradition states that when Muhammad was 12, he accompanied the Meccans' caravan to Syria. On this trip he met a Christian priest who is said to have foreseen Muhammad's career as a prophet of God. From this moment to Muhammad's revelation of the Hebrew God, there was relationship with the 'people of the Book'. Muhammad's foundational beliefs were that of the Eastern Christian community.

Following a lengthy period of Muhammad proclaiming this belief in Mecca, nearly 40 followers who recognised the God of the Christians as their God gathered together. This was followed by two emigrations called *"Hijrah*[15]*"*. The first emigration was due to the followers of Muhammad suffering under their fellow Meccans. They went to the area of Axun, which is in Ethiopia. The Christian king of this area, King Negus, represented a people that had centuries of Christian tradition dating back to the early centuries of the church.

Why did this migration move towards this Christian kingdom, if Christianity was a pagan religion according to Islam? On the contrary, the Ethiopian king responded to this group by saying, *"Jesus is just what you have stated him to be… Go to your homes and live in peace. I shall never give you up to your enemies."* This was at a time when the pagan Meccans were seeking physical *jihad* against the Muslims, however, the first Muslims lived under the protection and covering of the Christian Ethiopian king as he recognised they had a common faith!

This was the relationship Muhammad held throughout his lifetime with the Christian church, where, as protected minorities, they were recognized as the worshippers of the same God.

With this understanding, I have realised I have a family that I never knew I had. There has been a miracle in my heart, where

---

[15] *Moving from a land where a Muslim cannot practice his faith*

now I can sit in a room with Christians, laugh together, cry together, and see each other as brothers who have come from a common father.

When I pursued obedience to *Sharia*, there was never a moment when my heart was satisfied. I was never in a stage of peace. This is a strong contrast with today, where I can sit with my friends with a peaceful heart and rest at night with a peaceful mind.

Seeing the holy books with new eyes

Belief in the holy books from God is a foundational pillar of Islam. The Christian Scriptures are divided into three holy books for Muslims, which is confirmed by the *Qur'an*.

> *It is He Who sent down to thee (step by step),*
> *in truth, the Book, confirming what went*
> *before it; and He sent down the Law (of*
> *Moses) and the Gospel (of Jesus) before this,*
> *as a guide to mankind.*
> *(QS 3:3)*

The Holy Books revealed are the Taurat, Zabur and Injil (Old and New Testament) that have come from God. These Books are not the production of human wisdom.

The *Qur'an* was revealed to confirm what was revealed before, not to replace it. At the time of Muhammad, the Old and New Testament was not accessible or in the language for an Arab. In fact, the first person Muhammad went to at the time of his revelation of the God of Abraham being the true God, Waraqa bin Naufal, was attempting to translate the New Testament into Arabic.

As such, there are four holy books of Islam, including the *Qur'an*. Growing up, however, there was no comment or discussion beyond the Holy *Qur'an*. The previous revelation was placed in a corner, not to be discussed. This affected my religious understanding throughout my life. Concerning the Holy Books within Islam, there are three criteria that we were all taught. That is, to believe, receive and obey. These three criteria are followed for the *Qur'an*, but for the previous holy books, it is only believing that they are holy that is needed within modern Islam – receiving and obeying is not practiced for the Old and New Testament.

By seeing with new eyes, I now understand that Muslims *do not* embrace this as a pillar of faith in Islam. We are supposed to have faith in the previous revelation of God to be a Muslim, but what sort of faith does the modern Muslim have towards these Scriptures? I would suggest that we would not even be able to call it faith!

What is the reason behind rejecting the former revelations, the Old and New Testament? All levels of Islamic leadership generally teach that the *Qur'an* is the final revelation that cancels the previous. At the core of this is a very interesting situation. With Western Christianity claiming both the Old and New Testament as its own, there was an early movement amongst Arabs to claim and identify with the *Qur'an* as a distinct Arab holy book. It was not an issue of what contained truth and what didn't contain truth, it was an issue of cultural identity. However ultimately, the revelation Muhammad received predominantly contained the Hebrew Scriptures and pointed towards those scriptures.

As such, this rejection of the Old and New Testaments is a situation that contradicts the central mission of Muhammad. As I began to look beyond the issue of cultural identity, I began to embrace the truth that is contained within the Old and New Testament.

The Arab culture has a history of being a political enemy of the Roman Empire and its religion. When the former revelation that Muhammad pointed to, the Old and New Testament, was claimed to be the sole ownership of the Roman Empire, issues were created for Arabs. . For them, accepting the Old and New Testament essentially implied submission to the Roman Empire.

With my new eyes, I leave behind the politics of the past, and embrace the truth of the present, and realise that the Scriptures are not the ownership of a single political or religious group.

Seeing Jesus with new eyes

Growing up as a Muslim, I learned that Jesus was the 24th of the 25 prophets of Islam, and one of the greatest five prophets. However, what is expressed within the *Qur'an* is that the ultimate uniqueness of Jesus is incomparable with any other figure. Jesus' birth is explained in detail within the *Qur'an* itself, unlike any other prominent prophet. Jesus is declared as the one who is born of a virgin and who lived a sinless life. Jesus is declared as God's Word and as strengthened by the Spirit. This emphasis of the message of Muhammad is avoided within modern Islam. As with the recognition of the previous holy books, Muslims hold a fear of aligning their belief with their political enemy.

Now, as I look at my world with new eyes, I see the expression of God's love for mankind is through Jesus. Jesus' uniqueness according to Muhammad was that he was a sign of mercy for all mankind.

> *This is what your Lord says: It is easy for me, and this is so that we will make him (Jesus) a sign of mercy from Allah. This is a predestined matter.*
> *(QS 19:21)*

He was the channel for God's love and miraculous power, able to raise the dead. This is the clear belief of true Islam. For me, it was not just about *believing* in these truths that were there from the beginning days of Islam, but the main factor was *receiving* this truth personally.

Even beyond that, living in such a way that my actions reflect the life and instructions that Jesus left us with.

A journey from extremism to love

Part 3:

Sharia,
In a Different Time
and Place

Seeing the World
Through New Eyes

A journey from extremism to love

Chapter 9:
The Torah: A Foundation for Sharia

The word of God is spiritual, but it is received by a physical world. The physical things of our world can be torn up, burnt and destroyed. However the eternal things of God, His spiritual guidance and revelation cannot ever be destroyed.

God presented the law, that being the instructions for man to live in a blessed way, in a way that could be understood by the people it was presented to. His standards are unchanging, permanent and perfect. However when God's law is received in a local context, like Israel coming out of Egypt, God communicates His perfect standards in a way that is appropriate for their context.

In understanding the birth of Islam, and in particular the origin of *Sharia* Law that I endeavoured to impose upon all mankind, it is helpful to understand the Torah and the beginnings of the nation of Israel as they left Egypt. This is because of so many similarities in their context.

· Israel was a people who did not function as a nation; so was Arabia.
· Israel was without a law to govern it; so was Arabia.
· The beginning of the nation of Israel was in a desert context; so was Arabia.
· Israel had a prophet who endeavoured to build a nation based upon God's commands; so did Arabia.

God gave the Torah for the Israelites, and it was grace to those who received it. What I mean by this is that the Israelites undeservedly received the Torah from God to change transform them from a nation of slaves, to a prosperous and blessed people.

The revelation of the Torah to the Israelites was grace, as God graciously revealed what to eat, how to govern, and how to relate with one another in their context. This is why one of the great prophets recognized by Islam, David, delighted in the Law and in another of the Holy books of Islam, the Psalms, he expresses their thankfulness to God that the Torah was given to them as a nation.

For Christians, the idea of the Torah being perfect and an expression of God's grace seems to go against their foundational beliefs. When the word law is used, it usually has negative connotations, and is something to be applied to the wicked.

When God gave the Torah, His plan was for Israel to live a prosperous life if they obeyed His instructions. This was in contrast to the Jews in Paul's time, where the Torah was being imposed upon non-Jews as the basis for salvation. This was opposed by Paul passionately - the thought that mankind was saved by their works was something that was never intended by God! In writing to the Galatians, Paul says:

> What I mean is this: The law, introduced 430 years later, does not set aside the covenant previously established by God and thus do away with the promise. For if the inheritance depends on the law, then it no longer depends on the promise; but God in his grace gave it to Abraham through a promise.
> (Gal 3: 17 – 18)

God's promise for Israelites to be His people existed 430 years prior to the Torah being given to Moses. The Torah was given to God's people so that they would live a blessed life; it wasn't given for the purpose of inheriting God's mercy and becoming His people.

> But whose delight is in the law of the LORD, and who meditates on his law day and night. That person is like a tree planted by streams of water, which yields its fruit in season and whose leaf does not wither — whatever they do prospers.
> (Psalms 1:2-3)

*Blessed are those who fear the LORD, who find great **delight** in his commands.*
(Psalms 112:1)

The Hebrew people were to delight in God's instructions to them. It was a gift to them so that they could live a blessed life.

As were the people of Arabia in Mohammed's era, the Hebrew people were once a people that had no law. For 300 years they were slaves under the Egyptians Pharaohs. When God's time came for them to leave their life of slavery, the Hebrew's had grown to a population of about 3 million people.

It is hard to imagine this many people who had no infrastructure. There was no government to lead them, and they didn't have any land to call their own to settle. All they had was a covenant that God had made with their ancestors. As they traveled through the desert God said to them *"You are not a people, but I will make you a people."* (Deut 4:5)

The newly formed nation of Israel were totally dependent upon God's instruction. From the Torah, God's wisdom is expressed so to see a nation of slaves become a nation that is blessed and prosperous.

Beginning from that period, within 300 years God brought His people to be the most prosperous nation on earth. A queen, from the same region that Mohammed would later reside, heard of this nation that had become a great kingdom, and the Queen of Sheba came to see for herself.

> *She said to the king, "The report I heard in my own country about your achievements and your wisdom is true. But I did not believe these things until I came and saw with my own eyes. Indeed, not even half was told me; in wisdom and wealth you have far exceeded the report I heard. How happy your people must be! How*

> *happy your officials, who continually stand before you and hear your wisdom! Praise be to the LORD your God, who has delighted in you and placed you on the throne of Israel. Because of the LORD's eternal love for Israel, he has made you king to maintain justice and righteousness."*
> *(1 Kings 10: 6 - 9)*

The Torah which God gave to Israel covered every aspect of life, so that they could experience God's blessing. Often during this journey, the nation of Israel departed from God's instructions and their disobedience resulted in hardship. Despite much disobedience through the process, God had made Israel, by the time of Solomon, a Nation to be feared by all.

About 700 years after the Queen of Sheba admired the Nation of Israel, the Jewish religious leaders had transformed the following of the Torah into simply performing outward religious rituals, and as a means of suppressing the poor. Jesus was bringing Israel back to the purpose of the Torah which is loving God and loving your neighbour. In responding to the accusation that His teaching was in conflict with the Law and the Prophets, Jesus clearly showed that He was not here to undermine the authority of the Torah.

> *"Do not think that I have come to abolish the Law or the Prophets; I have not come to abolish them but to fulfil them. For truly I tell you, until heaven and earth disappear, not the smallest letter, not the least stroke of a pen, will by any means disappear from the Law until everything is accomplished.*
> *(Matt 5:17-18)*

Jesus' prayer for this world was for God's will be done on Earth like it is in Heaven. He desired that the standards of Earth would change to reflect those of Heaven. Why are the standards of God's people different to Heaven at the time of Jesus, when the standards of God's people originated from God at the time of Moses?*Did man change, or did God change?*

*"Why do your disciples break the tradition of the elders?
They don't wash their hands before they eat!" Jesus
replied, "And why do you break the command of God for
the sake of your tradition?*
(Matt 15:2-3)

Jesus, as a Jew, believed that the Torah came to Moses from God. However in addition to trying to pursue these instructions given by God, the people of Israel had also accumulated over 1,000 years' worth of traditions from the time of Moses until the time of Jesus.

The oral law, which was said to be the interpretation of the Torah by the 70 Elders in the book of Exodus, is what later became the Jewish Talmud. So in the time between Moses and Jesus, Israel followed (in varying degrees) both the written Torah (which was divided into the Books of the Law, the Prophets and the writings) and the oral Torah, which was transmitted verbally.

By the time of Jesus, traditions and the oral law had polarised the Jews into sects. Some believed the oral law was divinely inspired; some believed it was not to be followed. Jesus responded to one of these polarised groups, the Pharisees, by saying,

*" You have let go of the commands of God and are holding on
to human traditions."* And he continued, *"You have a
fine way of setting aside the commands of God in order to
observe your own traditions!"*
(Mark 7:8-9)

It was to those imposing these traditions upon others that Jesus quoted Isaiah, saying, concerning Israel's worship of God

*"They worship me in vain; their teachings are merely
human   rules"*
(Matt 15:9).

Jesus viewed these traditions imposed upon Israel as extra burdens that were not from God. For Jesus, obedience to God ought to be simpler and a matter of the heart (See chapter 14).

It was not only in regards to the oral traditions where Israel had departed from the original intent of the Torah in the time of Exodus. The written Torah was often interpreted by the Pharisees to suppress the people of Israel. In centuries prior to Jesus, David delighted in God's instruction that was the source of blessing to a nation. Now the Torah was being used as an instrument of religious leaders to suppress the masses!

> Then Jesus said to the crowds and to his disciples: "The teachers of the law and the Pharisees sit in Moses' seat. So you must be careful to do everything they tell you. But do not do what they do, for they do not practise what they preach.
> (Matt 23:1-3)

Jesus even recognised the validity of the Pharisees' interpretation of the written Torah. However of far greater importance than the teaching of the written instructions was living a life that was consistent with this message; not only that but having a heart that was changed and transformed.

> "Woe to you, teachers of the law and Pharisees, you hypocrites! You clean the outside of the cup and dish, but inside they are full of greed and self-indulgence. Blind Pharisee! First clean the inside of the cup and dish, and then the outside also will be clean."
> (Matt 23:24-26)

Confronting the hypocrisy of the Pharisees was another emphasis of Jesus, with the Pharisees observing minor rituals, but neglecting what is of real significance - matters of the heart. Jesus saw how far the religious culture was from the purpose of God as he revealed the Torah to His people.

The Torah gave instructions for the nation of Israel to live prosperously, and is a template, rather than a law, for the rest of the world to follow. God gave these instructions in the context of the Israelites leaving Egypt. From the most Northern people groups on the planet living in communities surrounded by ice, to some of the most southern people groups of Indigenous Australians, many of the commands given to the Israelites would not make sense in their context - the commands were for the specific situation of the Hebrews departing Egypt.

This leads us to a vital point of understanding the mission of the Prophet Muhammad and the beginning of Islamic Law. Understanding law for a local context in contrast with the universal commands that focussed upon the heart brought by Christ, (see Part 4) helps us better understand Islamic Law. Islamic Law was for a local context in Arabia. Despite context, Muhammad understood the Torah as the divine revelation of God which was his guide for the new Arab Tribal Federation.

The Arab peoples during the *Age of Ignorance (Jahiliyyah)* were in darkness: darkness covered their legal systems, religious systems and morality. Technology and development was non-existent. During this age, the law was on the side of the strongest: whoever was physically powerful ruled! That is the nature of tribal law.

At the time of the Prophet Muhammad, he hoped to build a theocracy, a nation that would live under God's standards. In that region during Muhammad's time, nomadic tribes lived under local laws and customs. Muhammad brought a reformation of law; it was a struggle of transition from the rule of tribal law to seeking a people group that lived under God's laws. It was a similar situation as Israel in the time immediately before and during the reign of King Saul.

This period was the start of Muhammad's tribe, the *Quraysh*, knowing and understanding moral law.

Seeing the World
Through New Eyes

A journey from extremism to love

Chapter 10:
The Arab Federation is formed

*T*he following two chapters have been gleaned primarily from the writings of William Montgomery Watt, in particular his books Muhammad at Mecca, Muhammad at Medina, and Muhammad: Prophet and Statesman. William Montgomery Watt is one of the world's most respected Western writers on Islam, both amongst non-Muslims as well as Muslims, in particular understanding the Prophet of Islam in his historical context.

In this chapter, we will look at how some of the traditions and laws of Islam were formed, particularly in areas that create misunderstanding for the West when removed from their historical context. We can totally misinterpret the story of Islam if we do not understand the context. With this chapter as a foundation, Chapter 11 will provide a chronological overview of the beginnings of Islam.

Nomadic Raids

Arabia and the surrounding areas in the time prior to Muhammad were not unified in any way. It was a region made up of nomadic tribes who viewed raids upon one another as culturally acceptable.

Generally, nomadic raids did not involve bloodshed. Their primary purpose was to take goods and camels, as the power of each tribe was reflected by the quantity of camels they held. The mark of a successful nomadic raid was the avoidance of bloodshed and conflict through the negotiating skills of the tribal leaders.

The occurrence of nomadic raids upon fellow tribes presents a background to the expansion of Islam in Holy *Jihad*, with the objective of *Jihad* not being bloodshed, but the effort to expand the Islamic faith and increase recognition of the God of Abraham.

At the time of Muhammad, each tribe of Arabia was loyal to its own group as a whole, not to a particular individual within it. The tribe was committed to unwritten customs that evolved, without being rooted in any particular religious or divine revelation, and any change to tribal law did not happen until the tribe as a whole embraced it. Honour within a tribe usually demanded that disputes between tribes were settled by force.

It is in this context of tribal nomadic life, tribal warfare, and the void of God-given law, that Muhammad came and declared his belief; that being, that there is no god but Allah. This statement was in opposition to the belief of tribal gods held by many tribes throughout Arabia, and an affirmation of the God worshipped by the Christians and Jews[16]. As we view the lack of legal structure within tribes, we have a greater appreciation for the instructions given on such a variety of subjects. These range from how a woman is to dress, to the penalty for fornication. The beginnings of Arabian law may appear random; however these instructions were to address constant, real situations faced by nomadic tribes as they were called to live under God's standards.

Federation of Tribes

It is this context of independent nomadic tribes which makes Muhammad's creation of an 'Arabian federation of tribes' impressive. This federation of tribes was later referred to as the 'Islamic state'. Again, we need to remember that those within this federation were those who had made a commitment to renounce their tribal deities and declare that there is no god but the Hebrew

---

[16]*The word "Allah" was generally used by Arabic speaking Christians for many hundreds of years prior to Islam in reference to God. Allah is closely link to Semitic languages such as Aramaic and Hebrew.*

God. What became known as the constitution of Medina[17], which was created by Muhammad, were detailed guidelines for all those tribes that had taken this step. Anyone who wanted to join this alliance was required to surrender to that God and accept this constitution. The followers of Muhammad in the beginning years of Islam recognised two types of people; one type of person being surrendered to the God of Abraham, and the other continuing in paganism and the worship of tribal deities.

With the formation of this alliance, the nomadic raids of one tribe against another ceased to occur. It was against the guidelines of the 'surrendered' tribes to carry out a raid on fellow tribes of the alliance. The passion that previously resulted in nomadic raids was redirected to become a passion to expand Islam, the surrender to the God of Abraham who is worshipped by Christians and Jews. When a tribal group was repeatedly targeted by raids, the attraction of forsaking deities and joining the federation greatly increased.

Within Arabia and the whole of the Middle East, there were numerous, isolated tribes of Jews and Christians who had diverse cultural practices and theologies. Christianity included those under the authority of Rome and the Chalcedonian creed, as well as those more culturally Hebrew who often recognised their roots back to the Jerusalem church. For all, scripture was predominantly oral in this era.

It was to these Christian tribes, primarily those not under Rome, that Muhammad gave the status of protected minorities.

These protected minorities were not Arabian Muslims, but Christians who were recognized as equal members of the federation, immune from attack, and viewed as worshippers of a common God. This is evidenced by numerous treaties that were made during this period. The most

---

[17] *A formal agreement between Muhammad and all of the significant tribes and families of Medina with the purpose of bringing an end the tribal fighting between the clans*

widely known of these within Islam is the Najran treaty in Saudi Arabia, which was a city-wide treaty with the Christian church. These treaties often had a common phrase, that being 'your God is my God.'

> *Only argue with the people of the Book (Christians) in a*
> *fair manner, except with the wicked amongst them. Say*
> *"We believe in what was revealed to us and revealed to you.*
> *Our God and your God is One, and we submit to Him.*
> *(QS 29:45- 46)*

In Muhammad's mind, the God of the Christians was his God! A part of Muhammad's Treaty with St. Catherine's Monastery, Mt. Sinai, Egypt, which is very similar with other treaties made with Christian settlements throughout Arabia, reads as follows:

"This is a message from Muhammad ibn Abdullah, as a covenant to those who adopt Christianity, near and far, we are with them. Verily I, the servants, the helpers, and my followers defend them, because Christians are my citizens; and by Allah! I hold out against anything that displeases them. Their Churches are to be respected. They are neither to be prevented from repairing them nor the sacredness of their covenants. No one of the nation (of Muslims) is to disobey this covenant till the Last Day (end of the world)."

At the time of Muhammad's death in 632 AD, the Islamic state comprised of about half of Arabia, which included a number of Jewish and Christian groups who had joined this federation as protected minorities.

Religion and Politics

The mindset of the Western world today in pursuing the separation of religion and politics has not been the mindset for the majority of history since Christ. In fact, within the church prior to the reformation, politics and religion has been very much intertwined. Wherever the Roman Empire expanded, sometimes by the sword, so Christendom expanded.

The beginning days of this occurred when Constantine made Christianity the official religion of the Roman Empire in 312 AD. When Rome fell in 476 AD, there were still no governments that had more power than the church. The Western Church controlled most of Europe, up until the Protestant Reformation in the 16th Century. It was this integration of religion and politics within Rome which Muhammad would have known about.

Just as religion and politics were closely integrated in Rome, so it was within Islam. The expansion of the Islamic state was the expansion of a political territory. In the early centuries, generally the people who became Muslims were formally pagans who had held to the worship of multiple deities, and who received an economic benefit in joining the federation. The conversion of these pagans meant that they could enjoy the benefits of being part of the alliance.

Generally within early Islam, it was not encouraged to seek converts amongst the protected Christian minorities. In fact, for a period of time, before the end of the 1st century of Islam, it was forbidden within Islam to convert Christians, because it would destabilize the economic foundation of the alliance. The protected minorities of those who recognized the God of Abraham contributed an annual tax to the federation in order to maintain this status as a protected minority.

Therefore, the fighting that contributed to the expansion of Islam, which was later referred to as *Jihad*, was not primarily aimed at the conversion of Christians, but was for the continued expansion of an alliance. The diverse groups of Christians in the Middle East were generally Hebrew oriented and resisted submission to the Catholic Church. Often for them, the alliance with 'The Federation of Arab Tribes' known as Islam was far more advantageous than aligning with the Roman Empire. With Islam, their churches and governance remained autonomous. This was in contrast to allegiance with the Catholic Church, where their churches ceased

A journey from extremism to love

Seeing the World
Through New Eyes   83

to be their own and they were subject to the regional Bishops to be a part of the universal church. One church leader speaks of his struggles under the Romans prior to Islam:

The Romans who throughout their dominions, cruelly plundered our churches and our monasteries and condemned us without pity.

God brought from the region of the south the sons of Ishmael (Muslims), to deliver us through them from the hands of the Romans. And if in truth we have suffered some loss, (because the Catholic churches, that had been taken away from us and given to the Chalcedonians); for when the cities submitted to the Arabs, they (Muslims) assigned to each denomination the churches which they found it to be in possession of.

It was no slight advantage for us to be delivered from the cruelty of the Romans, their wickedness, their wrath and cruel zeal against us, and to find ourselves at people.[18]

This presents the contrast of tax paying 'Protected Christian communities' who were able to maintain their autonomy, as compared to the position of the local church under Roman rule.

Character of Muhammad: Evaluated on what era?

The character of Muhammad has generally been a target of attack by the Christian church over the centuries. I would like to present that a key factor contributing towards this negative attitude is primarily the result of him being a leader of a political enemy of the Western Empire. Due to this, Muhammad was viewed as an enemy of the orthodox Christianity of his era.

One of the accusations against Muhammad is that his goal was to propagate a teaching that was contrary to the Bible, which he

---

[18] *Michael the Elder, Jacobite Patriarch of Antioch wrote this text in the latter part of the twelfth century, after five centuries of Muslim rule in that region*

himself knew to be false. We have already discussed the calling of Muhammad to introduce the Hebrew beliefs into pagan Arabia which resulted in a great personal cost to himself. It is only a true, genuine belief in what is being proclaimed that would explain Muhammad's willingness to endure hardship and persecution in a seemingly hopeless situation. Much of the leadership around him were men who were recognized as those of godly character, such as the respected Abu Bakar. If Muhammad was mistaken in some areas, we must conclude that he was genuine in his attempt to follow what he believed, and did not deliberately propagate a lie.

One of the other accusations common amongst Christians is concerning the moral values of Muhammad. He is accused as a lustful polygamous and child molester. The original context of Muhammad's multiple marriages following his 25 year marriage to Siti Khadijah can be observed in the following chapter. This is where we are to ask the question, do we judge Muhammad by the standards of our day, or his day? And if we judge Muhammad by the standards of our day, then we must also judge the attitude of American Christians prior to Martin Luther King Jr. concerning their attitude towards other races based on our standards today. At a minimum, we give grace to that era because of the cultural context that they lived in. That was 50 years ago. Muhammad lived 1,400 years ago amongst nomadic tribes of Arabia!

Understanding this historical context is in no way endorsing the deifying of Muhammad or the views that he was sinless. As clearly presented in our book "The Family I Never Knew I Had", Muhammad clearly declared himself as "Only a Messenger." Any deifying of Muhammad, and declaration of his perfection is contrary to the *Qur'an*.

Sharia formed for the Federation

The law of *Sharia* within Islam was instituted after Islam was formally recognized. One of the first places it was applied was in the holy city of Mecca, where Islam was first proclaimed, and where *Sharia* law was introduced to replace the pagan tribal laws which were embraced during the *Age of Ignorance*.

The context in which *Sharia* was given in is one of non-existent formal laws within the tribal setting. As such, it was revealed to instruct the everyday life of a Muslim. That means that *Sharia* was not only intended to instruct how to carry out prayers and fasting – its purpose extended to instruct in areas such as etiquette and hygiene. The foundation and template for *Sharia* was the Torah, which Muhammad recognized as the Divine commands given to Israel. This was to be the starting point for life's guidelines for nomadic tribes, who knew no formal law.

Sharia is by its nature not enforceable like Western law, due to its broad nature in giving instruction regarding daily private life. Because of this, the enforcement of *Sharia* in modern Islam is a source of confusion, as its original function was quite different. When Islam was proclaimed to Mecca, the Meccans initially rejected this message and the followers of Muhammad suffered for it. In this state of being persecuted, the prophet Muhammad and his followers migrated to Medina.

It was in Medina that laws and a kingdom were created for a community that was complex, multi-cultural, and deeply divided. This was the context in which *Sharia* Law was birthed.

Medina was somewhat dominated by Jewish factions in the era of Muhammad. These factions were most influential through their knowledge, rulership, religious tradition and trade. The Jewish community, which was often at war within itself, had strict religious law. In the formation of the laws for

Medina, the dominant influence was founded upon the Torah, because the Torah was already well established through the Jewish influence in Medina, and recognised by Muhammad, as the divine revelation of God for the guiding of a nation. The Jews of Medina claimed that their laws were universally the sole laws from God

> *So in this divided city, what were the laws from*
> *God to be for Medina?*

The Jews felt that if Muhammad wanted to join with them, he must pray the Jews' way and follow their rules. Messianic Jews had their own exclusiveness. To join the Christians, one had to submit to the Bishop, the Church of Rome, and to the creeds. There were many exclusive Christian sects and they all had their own initiation of joining: a baptism.

The culture of the Hebrews was not for another to baptize, but for self-baptism[19] And so it was this background that gave rise to the following quote from the *Qur'an*. I will give two different translations to emphasize a point:

> *Receive the baptism (Arabic: Sibgha) of God, and*
> *who is better than God in baptising? Him do we*
> *serve.*
> *(QS 2:138)*

> *We take our colour from God, and who is better than*
> *God at colouring. We are His worshippers.*
> *(QS 2:138)*

In the culture of exclusiveness that was present in Medina, where religious division was prominent amongst streams of Christianity and Judaism, Islam emphasized the "*Sibgha* of God". *Sibgha* means

---

[19] *An example of this can be seen on the Jesus Film, when Jesus baptizes himself*

"dye" or "colour".[20] The Arab Christians used to mix a dye or colour in the baptizing water to signify that the baptized person got a *new colour (transformed character) in life*. For Muhammad, baptism was the direct work of God Himself internally. It would seem a part of the reasoning for this was that method of baptism was such a divisive issue, that the following of a particular baptismal format would have put the Medina Constitution at risk.

To this day, baptism is a sensitive issue amongst Muslims. This sensitivity has its root in the beginning days of Islam, where baptism represented the changing of institutional or even political allegiances. My dream for Islam is that it would shake off the exclusiveness of the immigrants of Medina, and put on the colour of God, which can only be experienced through embracing the words of Jesus.

....

Sharia Law evolved in Medina in an environment of ethnic killings. What was to be the punishment for these killings? The dominant law of Medina was 'tooth for a tooth', to reflect the dominant citizens, Jews, and their influence on the newly formed kingdom.

The *Sharia* Law that was instituted for Medina became the foundation for other Arab communities, and later became the foundation for those who viewed *Sharia* as a global law for mankind to live by. We need to understand that the purpose of this law in its context was to bring unity amongst a multi-cultural community in Medina. It attempted to unify a city in recognizing the one true God of Abraham, despite there being differences of race and religion.

In that day, Islam was more of an attitude, not an institution, which brought people to leave behind the Age of Ignorance, and embrace the God of Abraham. It encompassed both Christians

---

[20]*Comment: Sibghah* ص ب غ: *the root-meaning implies a dye or colour; apparently the Arab Christians mixed a dye or colour in the baptismal water, signifying the baptized person got a new colour in life. Yusuf Ali.*

and Arabs. The purpose of Islam was a breaking down of exclusiveness. Jews maintained that there was no salvation outside of full obedience to their law, the Torah. Rome-centred Christians maintained that there was no salvation outside of the Catholic Church, and that anything culturally Hebrew was not to be included as a part of God's people, the Christian Church. Muhammad declared in Medina that surrender to God (Islam), no matter what religious allegiance, was the defining distinctive.

Islam in its formative years was primarily rejected by Jews because of its recognition of Jesus as the Messiah. This was one of the central doctrines opposed by the Jews. Beyond this, was the recognition by Islam of the *Injil* (New Testament) as the divine revelation of God, which would later become a pillar of Islam. This created a separation between the Muslim and the Jew that could not be overcome.

With a transformation within my heart, I can now see that the attempted enforcement of *Sharia* in this modern age is not a spiritual act, but is a continuation of the laws required for a newly formed local Arab kingdom in the 7th Century.

Many of the laws I attempted to impose upon others in my former life were not based upon a spiritual revelation or even from the Torah itself, but were from a specific human conflict that occurred in Arabia. Sarah and Hagar had a conflict that resulted in the driving out of Ishmael. This is interpreted as a foundational religious and spiritual truth; however ultimately it is simply a fight between two women.[21] It is the failings of mankind. As in the case of Sarah and Hagar, we make normal local conflicts into reasons why we can become religious enemies. This is not the problem of Medina law. This is not the problem of God; this is the problem of man's failings.

---

[21]The Apostle Paul specifically states "These things may be taken figuratively." (Gal 4:24)

Seeing the World
Through New Eyes

A journey from extremism to love

Chapter 11:
The story of Islam

The Meccan Context: A breakdown in tribal values

Shortly prior to Muhammad's time, Mecca had developed into a strategic trading gateway. Previously, the community of Mecca had still embraced the attitudes of the nomadic life in the Arabian Desert, which included maintaining strong tribal ties.

However a disintegration of tribal values had begun to take place in Mecca. Tribal members were increasingly materialistic and individualistic, leading to the oppression of those with lower social status, such as widows. For the average Meccan, it was an opportunity to increase power, wealth and influence. Previously, the poor were the responsibility of the tribe; now they were being neglected. Previously, honour for the tribe was paramount. In Muhammad's era, the obtaining of individual wealth and power replaced this.

We can see that early passages of the *Qur'an* address this specific situation.

The Gathering of Believers

Following Muhammad's initial revelation of the supremacy of the God of Abraham; he based himself out of a wealthy man's house in Mecca to share his message. At this point, in 614 AD, it is recorded that Muhammad was equipping and teaching 39 followers, based upon the revelation he had received. This mentoring continued for a number of years as they learnt for the first time to carry out acts of worship in bowing their forehead to the ground, to the God of Abraham.

This was in consultation with a Christian Bible translator who was translating the New Testament from Hebrew to Arabic.

This Bible translator, named Waraqa bin Naufal, was the first cousin of Muhammad's wife, Khadijah. As Muhammad and his followers, under the influence of Waraqa bin Naufal, continued to meet together daily, their whole belief system was being transformed from the pagan worship of the 360 deities in the *Kaaba*, to the formation of a Hebrew-influenced assembly that recognized the scriptures of the Christians as divinely inspired.

Appeal from the people of Medina

Opposition from the assembly in Mecca caused Muhammad and his followers to be somewhat ostracized. Muhammad's recognition of the God of the Christians left behind over 1000 years of Meccan tradition, which acknowledged all the deities in the *Kaaba*.[22] A departure from these deities put at risk the whole region of Mecca as a commercial trading centre. Every merchant that came to Mecca visited with the objective of presenting offerings to the deities in the *Kaaba*. Muhammad and his followers, through their Hebraic beliefs, threatened to destabilize Mecca's economy, somewhat similar to the effects of the Apostle Paul's ministry to Ephesus, which resulted in the silversmith craftsmen being affected by believers discontinuing worship of Artemis.

It is in this context that Muhammad received an invitation in 620 AD that would present new opportunities far beyond Mecca. Initially, 12 representatives from Medina were sent to

---

[22]*The Kaaba is a cube shaped building in Mecca, Saudi Arabia, and is one of the most sacred sites in Islam. It contained 360 idols, accumulated over hundreds of years. Muhammad later had the Kaaba dedicated to the worship of God alone and had all the other idols destroyed.*

Muhammad to explain the serious challenges facing Medina, as well as offering Muhammad a role to help solve these challenges. These 12 pilgrims from Medina, who travelled 250 miles, represented the 12 dominant ethnic groups who were at war with each other in Medina. Muhammad was seen as a neutral leader who did not have family ties with the warring tribes.

Two years later an additional representative party of 75 people from Medina arrived. They pledged themselves to accept Muhammad as God's messenger if he was to accept their invitation.

Troubles of Medina

Mecca and Medina were contrasting regions. Mecca did not have any agricultural industry, but it was a hub for trade. Medina was an oasis in the desert; prime farming land. It was extremely multi-cultural, with various Jewish ethnic groups having significant economic influence, as well as various Christian groups. Some were culturally Hebraic, and others were submitted to Rome. Beyond this, there were many traditional tribal groups within Medina that were considered pagan.

At the time of Muhammad's immigration to Medina, there had been a slow increase in ethnic violence for the past 100 years. With the dominant industry in Medina being agriculture, there were limited resources for the future wealth of each tribe. Clans had traditionally fought one clan against the other; however, increasingly there were alliances made and large-scale conflict erupted.

The complexity of this situation is indicated by position of the three dominant Jewish clans. They were a part of three separate alliances, clearly indicating this was not a conflict based on religious grounds, but rather on ethnic differences.

The urgency of Muhammad's invitation was caused by a major battle in Medina in 618 AD. This involved the majority of the clans in Medina and resulted in heavy casualties. From that year until the arrival of Muhammad, Medina was on alert.

Again, to read the *Qur'an* and understand *Sharia* we need to examine the context of Medina, which had no existing regional legal system to resolve ethnic disputes such as these.

The Hijrah (Emigration) of Muhammad to Medina, and the creation of Sharia

On July 16, 622 AD, Muhammad and his followers responded to the call of the Medinan tribes and took on the pilgrimage to Medina. The journey through the summer months of 622 AD was 250 miles, and it is believed to have taken a little under two weeks. The Islamic calendar today is calculated from the beginning of this journey.

Muhammad left behind only a handful of his followers in Mecca, including Abu Bakr, the respected godly man, who would later become Muhammad's successor.

First Months in Medina

Shortly after his arrival in Medina, Muhammad created what is now known as the Constitution of Medina. This provides evidence that the numerous warring multi-cultural clans now considered themselves as a single political unit under a Constitution that guided their actions. This document is very important when we look at the topic of *Sharia*. It is a Constitution that addressed the issue of ethnic violence. The multicultural population of Medina now referred to themselves as "*Ummah*[23]," which translates into English as "community".

---

[23]*The Muslim community*

The Constitution of Medina was a solemn agreement between tribes to form a federation together. Despite the rapid formation of this constitution, it would have been extremely difficult for the Medinan tribes to transfer loyalty from their tribe to an allegiance with their long-standing enemies.

It is this challenge that showed Muhammad's leadership. In this federation of tribes it would be incorrect to view Muhammad as the ruler. In fact Muhammad's followers, the emigrants from Mecca, were considered a distinct clan within themselves in Medina. Each clan continued to have their tribal ruler, and tribal rulers was governed by the solemn agreement of the Medinan Constitution.

It can be a struggle for the modern Western mind to understand this integration of religion and politics. The basis of Muhammad's success in Medina was his acceptance as a messenger of God, and the broad recognition that there are no deities except the God of Abraham.

Despite each clan's commitment to the Constitution of Medina, a number of Jews stood as opponents to Muhammad. The Jewish community was far from united as they were political enemies within themselves prior to Muhammad's coming. Additionally, Jews had limited knowledge of their religion and the Scriptures, with beliefs generally being transferred orally.

The Adoption of Jewish Practices by the Ummah

From the earliest days since Muhammad's initial revelation, Jerusalem was the Qiblah[24], which was the direction that Muhammad and his followers faced during prayer. More importantly, it was the direction that the Hebrew-orientated Christians continued to pray towards. For them, their source of hope, that being the Messiah, Christ Jesus, lived his life in this Holy City.

---

[24] *The direction of prayer, originally being Jerusalem but later, due to conflict, being directed towards the Kaaba (the sacred building at Mecca).*

As the federation in Medina entered its 2nd year, the position of Muhammad as God's messenger was far from being firmly established, and the religious practices of those in the *"Ummah"* were far from being fixed. The first non-exclusive place of worship in Medina for the *Ummah* was built by Muhammad for Friday prayers. However, neither the five daily prayer times nor the pilgrimage was established yet for Muslims. From the beginning, the religious practices of the *Ummah* were clearly Hebraic rather than Rome-influenced.

During Muhammad's time, the *Ummah* became the *'Jemaah'*[25] (religious assembly). This reflects a transition from a political agreement in which the people saw themselves as a loosely grouped community, to a people who saw themselves as a united people of God, under the ultimate authority of the God of Abraham.

Marriage and Expeditions

During the initial years in Medina, an important event took place in Muhammad's life. For the past 25 years, including the years in Mecca, Mohammad had been married solely to his first wife, Khadijah, a businesswoman from Mecca. However in 623 AD, he also made a commitment of marriage to A'ishah.

Monogamy was a rare exception in the Meccan culture, and beginning in Medina with Muhammad as a leader in a multi-cultural setting, he began to remarry a number of times, generally for politically strategic reasons.

A'ishah was one of these examples. She was the daughter of Abu Bakr, the respected leader who remained in Mecca. It was clearly a marriage that created strategic family ties. This followed a

---

[25] *Islamic Religious Assembly*

common Eastern tradition, where daughters were committed to marry kings for strategic relational alliances.

The Break with the Jews

The growing rift between Muhammad and many of the Jews had a number of driving factors. Muhammad based his position and beliefs upon the Pillars of Islamic faith that are held by Muslims to this day. This included recognition of the Old and New Testaments. The Jews clearly did not recognize the Christian Scriptures. They also pointed to contradictions in Muhammad's belief as compared to the Hebrew foundations. An issue with these debates was that they were primarily carried out based upon oral tradition, with written scriptures generally inaccessible in Arabic.

The revelation of the *Qur'an*, which during Muhammad's life was oral, insisted that its message confirmed the prior revelation held by Christians and Jews, and that the prophets of Islam were the same as the prophets of the Christians and Jews. When Jews who denied Jesus as the Messiah saw contradictions with their beliefs, this effectively undermined Muhammad's authority in Medina as a messenger from God, as well as the whole political stability of Medina.

As a solution to this clash with the Jews, Muhammad asserted that Islam, those being surrendered to the One True God, was embracing the God of Abraham. In this way if there was contradiction with the Jews, Islam was presented as purifying the original message that Jews had departed from. As previously stated, we need to remember that all of this debate was primarily based according to oral traditions.

The *Qur'an* is critical of the Jewish assertion that they are the chosen people. This again undermined the whole constitution of Medina, which could only be successful through a non-exclusivist approach. It is in this context that in February, 624 AD the Kiblah, which being the direction of prayer, was changed from Jerusalem to Mecca. Other changes in this time included the recognition of the month of Ramadan instead of the Jewish Day of Atonement.

These changes would affect the world to this day.

The 5 Pillars of Islam

The 5 Pillars of Islam are a requirement for every Muslim to carry out. This includes the Confession (*Shahadat*), the prayer (*Sholat*), the giving of alms (*Zakat*), fasting during *Ramadan*, and the pilgrimage to Mecca (*Hajj*). These were the requirements for me, and all Muslims.

Before I believed in the Bible, I understood these requirements originated from Mohammed and the birth of Islam. I thought that these requirements were according to Arab culture. But after I believed in the Bible message, I realised that these requirements of Islam did not have their origin from Arabia, but existed long before the proclamation of Muhammad.

The foundational confession, 'there is no God but Allah', reflects the confession of the Hebrews in the Shema, as well as the second of the Ten Commandments in having no other gods beside God. The pagan communities of Arabia had no way of knowing this foundational belief; there was no Bible in their language, and no messenger proclaiming it to them. This confession is the first requirement within Islam.

The other requirements of Islam, including the *Sholat* and fasting, also reflect Hebrew tradition. Moses and Jesus both prayed for extended periods of time. The journey to Mecca, the *Hajj*, was formerly to Jerusalem. I previously understood that all these requirements were founded in Arabia, but after I believed in the person of Jesus and received him, I realised that these practices have a background from Hebrew traditions.

For the Muslim world, the *Hajj* to Mecca is the ultimate journey. That was my experience when I visited Mecca numerous times, however if we are not careful, the journey and location itself can be object of worship, rather than God. We visit Mecca to remember the cleansing of idols from the *Kaaba*, but Mecca itself can become an idol in its place. On my previous trips I would meet people from nearly every nation on the planet who were fellow Muslims, and stay together with them in simple housing. But now, much of that has changed. Mecca today is a place of prosperity, which is a very different situation from the past.

The battle at Badr and Uhud

During the time that Muhammad was wrestling with his relationship with the Jews and transitioning worship rituals, a major issue was still yet to be dealt with. That was his relationship with his home region of Mecca.

In about 624 AD, a large Meccan trading convoy was on a journey to Medina. This would have been a significant opportunity for Muhammad to lead a raid, with the Meccans still devoutly pagan, and with no alliance existing between them and his followers who were committed to the one true God. At the same time, the emotions must have been greatly mixed within Muhammad, as a raid upon this convoy meant a raid upon his own ethnic people. We can only assume that amongst this group were potentially relatives and life-long acquaintances.

The raid on this convoy went ahead, which then became a catalyst for more significant action – the battle of Badr. In this event, 300 emigrants to Medina prepared themselves to battle with a large force of 950 men coming from Mecca. This was a turning point for the small Islamic army, as they defeated the larger force of Meccans, resulting in 50 prisoners being held, while the emigrants lost only 15 men.

The Muslims who had left behind the paganism of Mecca considered this as a great deliverance from God. It created a sense that God was for their cause, and was considered a 'sign' confirming Muhammad as God's messenger.

Within a year in March 625 AD, the battle of Uhud was underway, where the Meccan community sent out 3,000 men to seek retaliation. At this time, Muhammad was still struggling with his relationship with the Jews of Medina, and they chose not to align themselves with him in this battle. Consequently, Muhammad branded them as hypocrites.

The battle of Uhud is the background of numerous passages in the *Qur'an*, including 3:159-160

If you are determined, trust Allah. Allah loves those who trust Him. If Allah saves you, none can defeat you. If he deserts you, who can save you then? Let the believers trust Allah!

Despite the defection of Jews from Muhammad's army, the federation of Arab tribes under Muhammad fought with a total of 700 men. Although the Meccans had a much larger army, their troops were not well-trained. The conclusion of the battle of Uhud, according to numerous scholars, is divided as to who was victorious. However, at a minimum, it was a significant moral victory for the Muslims.*New Horizons*

Throughout political expansion of Medina, for Muhammad, what reigned supreme was the calling of Arab tribes to the God that Christians worshiped – the God of Abraham. Despite the political challenges of maintaining unity in Medina amongst diverse Arab tribes, this issue was secondary. 'There is no God but Allah' was the ultimate unifying declaration.

Despite the two major battles with the Meccans, by 625 AD Islam had still only called pagan tribes around Medina and Mecca to monotheism. However, the vision of Muhammad was for the entire Arabian peninsula to be a united federation of tribes, that would leave paganism entirely and recognise that there is no ruling deity except that which was introduced by the Hebrews.

On the 13th of March, 628 AD, a historic event took place. Following a peace treaty with Mecca, Muhammad was able to take a pilgrimage to this city, which is called until this day *Umrah*[26] or 'The lesser pilgrimage'. He called on Muslims to bring animals for a sacrifice in Mecca, remembering the sacrifice of Abraham, with approximately 1500 men taking this pilgrimage from Medina.

In being able to negotiate a 10 year peace treaty with Mecca, it was in effect, the ceasing of war with this city and a period of major strengthening for the Muslim community.

Mecca's Surrender

A year later, Muhammad journeyed once again to Mecca for the lesser pilgrimage, with approximately 2000 men from Medina. However during this time the peace treaty was put into jeopardy because of an old tribal conflict that flared up.

In order to negotiate a compromise with Muhammad, one of the Meccan leaders, Abu-Sufyn, left to Medina. At this time, Mecca was in no position to face the army of Medina. A peaceful surrender of Mecca was pursued – perhaps related to the strategic marriage that had already taken place between Muhammad and Abu-Sufyn's daughter.

---

[26] A pilgrimage to Mecca, Saudi Arabia, performed by Muslims that can be undertaken at any time of the year

On the 1ˢᵗ of January, 630 AD, Muhammad led his army from Medina with approximately 10,000 men. Abu-Sufyn and leading Meccans formally met Muhammad and as a region, they committed to forsaking their traditional deity worship, and from that point on, live a 'life of Islam' to God. In return, Muhammad immediately recognized Mecca as a part of the community of Islam, with Muhammad remaining in Mecca for approximately three weeks with his army.

The implications, emotions and historical significance of these three weeks must have been dramatic, as the deities housed in the *Kaaba* were destroyed, and the *Kaaba* itself became recognized as a location of worship to the God of Abraham. This was the moment when over 1000 years of tradition would be changed!

The Ruler of the Federation of Arabia

Mecca left behind its pagan worship, and embraced monotheism. In one sense, this did not make a major difference to Muhammad's position in Medina. The emigrants of Medina were still considered as a distinct tribe with Muhammad as its leader, and all tribal leaders of the region continued to be submitted to the Constitution of Medina.

The greatest impact of Mecca embracing monotheism and the community of Islam was that it increased the number of pagan tribal leaders who approached Muhammad to join the Arab alliance. Distinct tribes could have ranged from small villages to large towns. This integration required a great knowledge of the tribal structures and cultures within the region. It was here that Muhammad's second-in-charge, Abu-Bakr, was vitally important. He had knowledge of these areas beyond that of anyone else.

The federation of Arab tribes risked being divided and broken up through tribal allegiances. Often tribal leaders were recognized as deity-type figures. In response to this, the testimony required to join the federation included recognizing Muhammad as a messenger of God - as their authority, but only as God's appointed messenger.

Syahadat (Confession)
Are we making the status of Muhammad the same as God?
Ismail Yasin

لا إله إلا الله محمد رسول الله

There is no god but God, and Muhammad is his messenger.

This simple confession is the door into Islam. Every Muslim is required to say this as a part of their religious requirements. The first part of this confession, *"There is no god but God"*, is foundational for the Islamic faith, as has already been discussed. The second part of this confession, *"And Muhammad is his messenger"*, is also an important part that cannot be separated.

There was a time when I was seriously considering statements that questioned this confession, shown to me in books or discussed in conversations with non-Muslim friends. They said "If God is the centre of focus for Muslims as the one true God who is to be worshiped, why do you need to have a statement that must be confessed acknowledging Muhammad as his messenger? Doesn't this compromise the first statement, and put Muhammad at the same level as God?" This was followed by another question, "Is Muhammad a prophet?"

If we seriously look at the *Qur'an* and think about the two parts of this confession, we would realise that this is not putting Muhammad on the same level as God. In fact, it is absolutely the opposite! With clarity the *Qur'an* states that Muhammad is not God, but only his messenger who God sent to the Arabs. *"There is no god but God"*; this cancels the thought immediately that Muhammad is god. This is explained in Ali Imram 144:

> *Muhammad is no more than a messenger: Many were the messengers that passed away before him.*
> *(QS 3:144)*

The confession was an important platform to deal with the customs of the *"Age of Ignorance" (Jahiliyyah)* in the Arab world during Muhammad's time. The tendency during this time was to make their tribal leader into a cult figure. Therefore in the original message that Muhammad brought, there was a very clear defining line so that the focus would be upon one God:

> *Say (unto them, O Muhammad): I am only a warner, and there is no god but God, the One, the Absolute.*
> *(QS 38:65)*

This verse very clearly explains that Muhammad is only a messenger! If a Muslim recognizes Muhammad as more than that, then they are not following the *Qur'an*. If a Muslim is true to this instruction, we can say we are proud of our Prophet because according to this revelation, he was often reminded of who he was. I am sure he was well aware of the customs in tribal life of lifting up a leader as a god, as this verse well explains.

The confession of Muhammad as a messenger also emphasizes the urgency for the proclamation of the message. Who would receive the message if the messenger is not recognized? As an example, we can see in the life of Jesus that teachers of the law and Jewish leaders were often opposed to Him. Many of them rejected what Jesus proclaimed, even accusing him that his miracles came from the power of the devil, because they could not accept that the son of a carpenter from a small town in Nazareth was the Messiah sent from God; the Word that became flesh! In a similar way Muhammad, in his mission of proclamation to the Arab world during the *Age of Ignorance,* faced opposition due to his social status and tribe.

Those following the message that Muhammad brought through the *Syahadat*[27] were defining a) The position of God as supreme, b) The Messenger as nothing *more* than a Messenger, and c) A declaration that despite his social status and opposition from those who held on to gods, that he was given a special role in pointing Arab people to the God of Abraham.

....

The World Empires at the time of Muhammad

Roughly during the time of the Emigration *(Hijrah)* of the Muslims from Mecca to Medina, a number of global changes were occurring amongst the dominant world empires. In one of these events, the Persians (from modern day Iran), attempted an attack upon Constantinople in 626 AD. Constantinople represented the headquarters for the Eastern Roman Empire and the Catholic Church. The attempt by Persia was unsuccessful and resulted in a decline in the success and power of the Persian Empire.

Muhammad would have been well aware of these major global events. In fact, it had immediate and local repercussions for many Arab tribes that were *pseudo-states of the Persian Empire* throughout Arabia. Consequently, these tribes were no longer able to support or govern themselves without the backing of the Persian Empire.

Many of these formerly Persian-aligned Arab tribes turned to the federation of Arab tribes in Muhammad's time. By 630 AD, the Persian Empire was disintegrating faster than any had anticipated, virtually disappearing within a decade, and Muhammad effectively became an heir to the Persian Empire.

---

[27] The confession

He had an increasing interest in the expansion of the federation. This led to what is probably regarded as the greatest of Muhammad's expeditions, that being to the Gulf of Akaba, at a place called Tabuk, during the months of October to December 630 AD. It was by far the greatest army that Muhammad had led during his lifetime, totaling 30,000 men. Numerous treaties were implemented with small Christian and Jewish communities along the way, guaranteeing them protection upon their payment of the annual tax.

This arrangement was intended to be a permanent, ongoing partnership. This was one of the central aspects of the Islamic empire, where Christian communities were acknowledged as protected minorities, with the first part of the Muslim creed (Shahadat), that is, "There is no deity but God" a confession for all within the Federation, whilst the second part of the Islamic confession, that Muhammad is His Messenger, being required of those joining the federation of Arab tribes who had left behind paganism. Whether fully Muslim, or protected minorities, all would be under the protection of "God and his Messenger", that is the Islamic state.

As a protected minority, Christians were allowed to manage their own internal affairs, in addition to holding full control and ownership of assets. This relationship Islam held with Eastern Christianity contrasted with Eastern Christianity under Rome, where ultimate authority and assets became the ownership of the universal Catholic Church.

With the expansion of the federation of Arab tribes, the quick surrender of pagan communities resulted in a greater financial benefit for that community. The early centuries of Islam presents a good record of toleration towards minorities. This was because the name of Muhammad as God's messenger, and the name of the movement itself were at stake. A commitment to treaties was essential for future treaties to be implemented. However as centuries passed, and a breakdown of these treaties, beliefs and attitudes took place, there was no other system to replace it - resulting in political instability throughout the Middle East.

The Extent of Muhammad's Power

The federation of tribes in 632 AD had its core alliance around Medina and Mecca. By this time Muhammad had greatly unified the Arabs, despite there still being diverse language and culture. With this federation, monotheism became the foundation for unity and belief. The federation attracted nomadic tribes for various reasons. It could have been the protection from nomadic raids, or it may have been the significant trade advantages joining the alliance.

Ultimately, the message of Islam was that all within its federation were equal, evidenced now by the common ritual on the *Haj* [23]. Allegiance to the federation also meant a tribe didn't have to be subject to a distant power, whether that is a Persian or Roman power.

As both the Persian and the Byzantine powers opposed each other and began to disintegrate, the tribes that aligned themselves to these powers needed something to provide them stability. This was one of the key attractions of Islam.

In March 632 AD, Muhammad led himself on a pilgrimage to Mecca. Previously this pilgrimage was for protected minorities as well, but it now became a celebration for Arab tribes who had embraced monotheism. The 632 AD pilgrimage was the final one for Muhammad. Returning to Medina in poor health, he passed away on 8th June, 632 AD.

In the midst of confusion upon the passing of their leader, Abu

---

[28] The Haj is one of the largest pilgrimages in the world, and one of the five pillars of Islam

Bakr, the ultimate successor of Muhammad, rose up and stated, "O ye people, if anyone worships Muhammad, Muhammad is dead, but if anyone worships God, He is alive and dies not."

In a culture where Arab tribes often worshiped tribal leaders as deities, a change had taken place. Muhammad's message was that he was only a messenger, and now that he was gone, their worship would continue towards the God of Abraham.

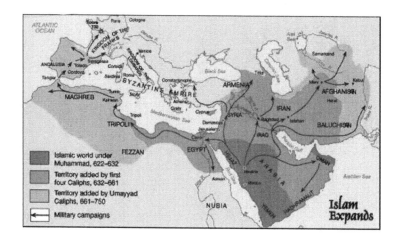

Part 4:

The Universal Law
For the Heart

A journey from extremism to love

Chapter 12:
Returning to the heart

The place where God interacts with us is the heart. Whether I *sholat* in the mosque, or fast, or give, the key place is my heart. This small intimate place is at the centre of the human life. Our worship can begin in the majestic *Masjid al-Haram* (The Grand Central Mosque) in Mecca, or at a small simple rural mosque, or at a simple synagogue, at a big cathedral, or a small local church building, but the meeting place with the Spirit is in this quiet, small location called the heart.

I had a transformation of my heart where God's Spirit dwells. That is the majesty of the human heart. The human heart is beyond the majesty of the *Masjid al-Haram*, or the Great Temple in the era of Jesus. To focus on the physically majestic places of prayer does not create a heart that is pure. No matter what the grandness the location of worship, it is the changed human heart that changes our destiny.

The goal of our physical world is the pursuit of physical riches, but the goal of the Kingdom of Heaven is a changed heart. When we leave this physical world, the bodies of both the rich and the poor will return to the same dust. All our riches will be left behind, and we will be judged according to our heart.

Although it is of critical importance, it can be easy to overlook matters of the heart and focus on the material or physical things in our life. This can be seen clearly in the lives of the Pharisees of Jesus day, who often came to Jesus regarding dilemmas of obedience to the written law, similar to modern *Sharia* Law. As I endeavoured to do, the Pharisees often focused more strongly on the actions necessary to follow a law, rather than on the intention, heart and purpose of it. A number of the questions they posed to Jesus related to the Sabbath, particularly healing on the Sabbath.

> He said to them, "If any of you has a sheep and it
> falls into a pit on the Sabbath, will you not take
> hold of it and lift it out? How much more
> valuable is a person than a sheep! Therefore it is
> lawful to do good on the Sabbath."
> (Matt 12:9-14)

This statement was opposed by the Pharisees, who maintained
that such actions violated Sabbath law. In this situation, Jesus
explained that there is a greater law that is to embraced. It flowed
from the heart, the law of love and compassion.
It is in this context that Jesus explains,

> "The Sabbath was made for man, not man for the
> Sabbath"
> (Mark 2:27)

For Jesus, the issue was not obedience to the law, and how to
successfully come up with an answer so as to be obedient within
complex ethical situations. Jesus views the Law as having a centre
and a periphery. For Jesus, obedience to the Law naturally flows
from a pure heart, so that, if the heart is pure, the Law will be
fulfilled.

> "The eye is the lamp of the body. If your eyes are
> healthy, your whole body will be full of light.
> But if your eyes are unhealthy, your whole body
> will be full of darkness. If then the light within
> you is darkness, how great is that darkness!
> (Matt 6:22-23)

Jesus highlights matters of the heart as the origin of true obedience to
the law in such a way that the Pharisees and many other Jews could
not accept it. Obedience to the written law in external actions only
was a stepping stone that could lead to hypocrisy. This external focus
had the ability to leave the heart completely untouched!

In contrast to this, the focus upon the internal – the heart – that Jesus brought, meant that a person's actions and words were changed from the inside out rather than by being 'managed' by external obedience. Ultimately this resulted in de-emphasising physical rituals, and putting a focus upon that which is unseen.

Jesus confronted this kind of hypocrisy regularly. He lived in a time and place where there were some segments of Judaism that disregarded matters of the heart, and sought righteousness by maintaining outward appearances. Jesus objects to the Pharisees who made great efforts to appear righteous externally. He says of them,

> *"Everything they do is done for people to see."*
> *(Matt 23:5)*

Jesus referenced examples of giving money for show; he states that rather than making it a public event, giving should be done in private. In regards to fasting, Jesus again stresses the importance of practicing this in secret, rather than making it known to others to maintain the appearance of spiritual superiority. Although undertaking 'righteous' actions; these same people were disregarding the heart of the law, resulting in unrighteousness in their own hearts.

In the same way, my own heart was left untouched and overlooked in all my years spent pursuing the implementation of *Sharia* Law. I was diligent in obeying Islamic law, but my heart was hidden from everyone. However as truth got hold of me, it was my heart that became the focus of my spirituality, being cleansed by the ultimate sacrifice – Jesus blood - that was the only solution to my sin.

A journey from extremism to love

Chapter 13:
God leads us in His standards, not man

Man is greatly influenced by the commands he perceives are from God. Pursuing that which is commanded, and fleeing that which is forbidden; that is what we endeavour to do. It is a vital part of the mindset of man.

Some people believe that Jesus did away with specific standards to live by, as his followers left the law and lived under grace. However the greatest command left by Jesus to his followers was to teach peoples around the world to do all that he commanded. In fact much of the New Testament is advice to flee from actions that break the commands of the Torah, such as adultery.

The *Sharia* Law that I attempted to enforce mankind to live under did not necessarily contradict standards that many genuine Western Christians embrace. For example, *Sharia* Law encourages modesty, and it discourages alcohol use. In fact, *Sharia* Law generally reflects the standards that Jesus observed Himself, including laws relating to food.

If this is the case, why doesn't the modern application of *Sharia* Law generally produce a community of love that was modelled by Jesus? This Law neglects the heart and overlooks the work of the Spirit. Previously, my whole attempt to follow God's will and His commands were through my own efforts, and I endeavoured to impose this upon others. In this, I was mistaken with an essential element of truth. I needed to understand the frailties and limitation of man, which needed to submit and surrender to God's Spirit in guiding me in his standards. The inspiration was to be from God, not from man. This is what has been transformed in my understanding.

> *The Spirit gives life; the flesh counts for nothing. The words I have spoken to you – they are full of the Spirit and life.*
> *(John 6:63)*

In following God's will, it is God that gives me life, not my own efforts of obedience, which become a source of pride. I am someone who falls short of his standards, but He is the one who enables me to be changed. This means that there should be no room for pride based upon my actions.

When the Spirit of God leads us, He leads us towards what God desires. This is exemplified in Jesus. Every action of his life was not his own will, but God's. His words, his actions, the totality of his life were not his efforts but the Spirit of God. We can see this demonstrated in the following verses:

> *"The Spirit of the Lord is on me, because he has anointed me to proclaim good news to the poor.*
> *(Luke 4:18)*
>
> *Jesus returned to Galilee in the power of the Spirit*
> *(Luke 4:14)*

Therefore, I needed to change my thinking. Who is the one who changes and guides me, God or myself? If I am to follow the example of Jesus, it is the Spirit of God within that moves me towards God's standards. He is the one who leads me to truth, the one who leads me to the path of life, the one who reveals light; it is through God's Spirit, not me. Outside of God's enabling, we do not live in faith. The laws of the world focus upon the outward actions; however God's Spirit changes the heart.

When Jesus walked this earth; he was directly revealing the "Torah" of God through his own mouth, which is the instruction from God on how to live. Before Jesus left, he instructed his followers that he himself would later not be physically present with them, but God's presence would be guiding them in how to live according God's standards. For those who lived after the era of Jesus, if they were not guided by God's Spirit, they would fail in living according to His standards.

In my former paradigm, I tried to act according to the law that was revealed to Muhammad, who endeavoured to base his law upon the Torah. However, my actions were independent of the Spirit promised by Christ. I saw the law, but I did not know God's voice.

Why is there the command, "Do not murder"? A command is only given to someone if there is a tendency to carry out that action. Our flesh wants to respond to wrong-doing with revenge. The heart of man has a tendency to disobey God, not to lead fellow man into righteousness. We are dependent upon God's Spirit to lead us in righteousness.

Without the guidance of the Spirit, the following of God's standards becomes a ritual. With ritual, when we are tired we have no motivation to follow the written law. When following the law seems to limit us, we leave it. With the Spirit, the Spirit doesn't get tired, whether we are in a lonely place, or a busy place, in any context the Spirit continues to be able to guide us.

Seeing the World
Through New Eyes

A journey from extremism to love

Chapter 14:
The Heavenly Kingdom

God revealed to us the eternal, heavenly law through Jesus. "The Kingdom of Heaven is like..." was an often-repeated message of Jesus. To receive the message of Jesus, we receive that which is spiritual, not physical. We receive that which is universal, not local, and that which is eternal, not temporal.

The core of Jesus' teaching is that the kingdoms of this world would reflect heaven; 'Your *kingdom come, Your will be done, on earth as it is in heaven*'.

We should not impose traditions and laws from earthly kingdoms upon others. This is the misinterpretation of *Sharia*, that the law for Arabia was a requirement for all of mankind. This same misinterpretation can also be true of many Christians, for whom the standards and practices of Western Christianity become the universal standards of the kingdom of heaven!

On the contrary, we are to receive the heavenly values and standards revealed through Christ, which are to be reflected within earthly kingdoms, whether that be Israel, Saudi Arabia or the USA.

The commands of Christ went beyond the physical to reveal the Kingdom of Heaven. When we judge another person's form of prayer, the person judging is implying that they have a form of prayer that is universal and that is from Heaven. However the kingdom of Heaven is beyond outward rituals. If a Christian judges me when I *sholat*, it implies a recognition of the Christian ritual of prayer as the universal form of praying, as opposed to Jesus presenting the law of the Kingdom of Heaven, where the essence is beyond the physical. Whether prayer, fasting or giving; Jesus revealed the essence of the heavenly law that goes beyond any local physical standard.

Jesus was led by the Spirit, not by the focusing on the laws written in ink. The evidence of this was that when He spoke, He spoke with authority; He laid his hands on the sick and they recovered; He drove out demons. Could someone who simply follows written instructions carry out these things?

The fact that the crowds were shocked that Jesus spoke with authority implies that the teachers of the law did not speak with authority. The simple following and implementation of the law by the Pharisees did not contain this same authority.

When we come to religious tradition and ritual, the heavenly eternal law revealed by Christ says don't pray in front of others so that you can respected, but pray in a hidden place. This presents one aspect of prayer according to the Kingdom of Heaven. However many of the traditions and rituals for prayer we see today are according to local contexts. For example, we might pray in a nice religious building that is highly ornamented, as the building endeavours to reflect a holy place. Or we may pray in a mosque. The religious leader might wear clothing that reflects a level of holiness, whether that be a long beard or a cross.

All of this is striving to present a physical, local setting as a holy place. This is based upon the physical paradigm, attempting to give the impression of a local context that this is heavenly, so that we can receive a response from God. However, this doesn't necessarily contain the essence of heavenly prayer.

Despite focussing upon the unseen rather than the seen, this does not mean that Jesus did away with the Torah. In fact, Jesus was challenging his followers about obedience to God's standards. He said to them;

> *Not everyone who says to me Lord, Lord will*
> *enter the kingdom of Heaven, but only those who*
> *do God's will*
> *(Matt 7:21)*

For I tell you that unless your righteousness
surpasses that of the Pharisees and the teachers
of the law, you will certainly not enter the
kingdom of heaven.
(Matt 5:20)

Rather than doing away with the law, Jesus intensified the focus upon its intention and revealed the eternal essence of the Law. For example, at the time of Jesus, the teachers of the Law said, "Do not commit adultery." Did Jesus do away with this law? No, he intensified its application by teaching that if you even *think* adulterous thoughts, you have already committed adultery. The teachers of the Law said, "Do not murder". Jesus responded, "*Anyone who is angry with his brother will be subject to judgement.*"

Did Jesus do away with the Law? No, rather he brought the application of it to a whole new level. He was bringing the matter back to the origin of external actions, that being the heart. And the heart needed to be transformed.

In my former paradigm as an implementer of modern *Sharia*, my actions originated from my heart. From there it was confessed by my mouth, and finally, if I was bold enough, *Sharia* was carried out with action. The problem was, my heart needed a transformation. The *Sharia* Law that I followed was focused upon the action, but was powerless to transform the heart.

Despite Jesus bringing the application of the Law to a whole new level, the commands of God are not intended to be a heavy yoke. On the contrary, the instructions of God as Jesus understood were light and easy.

Come to me, all you who are weary and
burdened, and I will give you rest. Take my yoke
upon you and learn from me, for I am gentle and
humble in heart, and you will find rest for your

souls. For my yoke is easy and my burden is
light.
(Matt 11:28 – 30)

God's commands were intended to enable people to live a blessed life. God is not a hard task master, but He is as a most loving and most compassionate father. This foundational understanding of God held by Muhammad has not been embraced or understood by Muslims.

The Ten Commandments can be divided into two categories that are to be obeyed. Firstly, there are the actions that we do in our service to God, and secondly, our actions in service to mankind. Our commitment to God is reflected by our commitment to fellow man. When you are committed to God with your whole being, you will be committed to and love your fellow man as you love yourself. This summarises the essence of the law from the Torah, which had long since been forgotten by the time of Jesus. When this commitment and love is fulfilled there is no law in the Torah that you break. This is a central theme of all the New Testament writers:

> *For the entire law is fulfilled in keeping this one command:*
> *"Love your neighbour as yourself".*
> *(Gal 5:14)*

As implementers of modern *Sharia* Law, Islam has failed to live out the essence of Heavenly law. Why? Firstly, it has not understood the heart of the law that can be summarised by loving God with your whole heart and loving your neighbour as yourself. Secondly, *Sharia* is outworked by man's efforts, rather than being led by God.

The Word became Flesh

In former times, God spoke to His people through the Torah to bring them out of slavery into a blessed life. In these last days, God has spoken to mankind through Jesus so as to bring life, and life abundantly.

> *Christ Jesus the son of Mary was a Messenger of God, and His Word, which He bestowed on Mary.*
> *(QS 4:171)*

The *Qur'an* states that Jesus *is* God's Word. This is despite efforts of *Qur'anic* translators to conceal this truth by presenting Jesus as having been created *by* God's word. At the time of Jesus, confusion reigned as to how mankind was supposed to live. In Jesus, God's Word became tangible in a way never known before.

> *The **Word** became flesh and made his dwelling among us.*
> *(John 1:14)*

At the time of Jesus, God's Word in the Torah was vague and distant for the people of Israel. Through Jesus, God revealed His word in a personal way, to reconcile the world to Himself. God was doing a new thing.

> *I will raise up for them a prophet like you from among their fellow Israelites, and I will put my words in his mouth. He will tell them everything I command him. I myself will call to account anyone who does not listen to my words that the prophet speaks in my name.*
> *(Deut 18:18-19)*

For Moses said, 'The Lord your God will raise up
for you a prophet like me from among your own
people; you must listen to everything he tells
you. Anyone who does not listen to him will be
completely cut off from their people.
(Acts 3:23-23)

Peter recognised in Acts 3:23 that God's promise of sending a prophet
who would be His mouthpiece was fulfilled in Jesus. In these verses
we can recognise the importance of not just confessing Jesus as the
Christ, but truly hearing his words. Referring to Jesus as a Prophet is
commonly avoided or overlooked within Christianity. Islam refers to
Jesus as a prophet, which is what God said he would be to Moses.
However Jesus was a unique prophet, in being God's *Kalam* (Word).
John the Baptist confirmed this when he said of Jesus, *"He whom God*
has sent speaks the words of God" (John 3.34). Jesus is not just one who
received the Word; He is what the Word became. He is the living,
breathing, walking word of God.

*The **word**s I say to you I do not speak on my own*
authority. Rather, it is the Father, living in me,
who is doing his work.
(John 14:10)

*These words you hear are not my **own**; they*
belong to the Father who sent me.
(John 14:24)

Islam represents those who have surrendered themselves to God's
Kalam (word). Jesus is unique according to Islam compared to any
other prophet that lived. This uniqueness of Jesus according to the
Qur'an originated from God. Because of that, the unique Christ
must be believed and received. In believing and embracing Christ
it means our heart, followed by our confession, followed by our
actions, in other words our whole totality, are to be influenced by
Christ. As believed by the messenger of Islam, Jesus is the
expression of God's mercy. Jesus is the Word of God that gives life,

with his words needing to be embraced to experience true life. Muhammad understood Jesus as the Word of God - the Word that revealed and contained the true nature of what God was like.

The life of Jesus was a renewed understanding and revelation of God's love and compassion for mankind. The New Testament writers, in summarising the Torah as "Loving God and your Neighbour," recognised that God's love was a reality during the era of the "Teachers of the Law and the Prophets." However, through the transferring of God's revelation from Moses to Jesus, the essence of who God is was totally lost. And so, in these last days God speaks not through the writing on of tablets, and his presence is not through the Holy of Holies in the Tabernacle, but He speaks to us through Christ.

God's Word now is alive and present amongst mankind. His Word has become flesh! His Word dwells amongst us.

....

The Church and the Torah
(Daniel Roberts)

Since the early centuries of Christianity, a common view has been that the Torah and Israel has been replaced and superseded by the New Testament and the Christian Church. That which was Hebrew was considered superseded and even cursed. Over the centuries, official church statements were made concerning this, such as the following:

> *In one word, I renounce absolutely everything Jewish*[29]

---

[29] ^ Parks, James (1974), *The Conflict of The Church and The Synagogue*, New York: Atheneum, pp. 397–98.

Amongst other terms, this is known as "Replacement Theology", where the Hebrew peoples were replaced as God's people by the Gentile church, which was the Catholic Church. Replacement Theology is where essentially the West replaced the East. (A more thorough explanation of the History of this can be read in Appendix 1)

> [17] If some of the branches have been broken off, and you, though a wild olive shoot, have been grafted in among the others and now share in the nourishing sap from the olive root, [18] do not consider yourself to be superior to those other branches. If you do, consider this: You do not support the root, but the root supports you. [19] You will say then, "Branches were broken off so that I could be grafted in." [20] Granted. But they were broken off because of unbelief, and you stand by faith. Do not be arrogant, but tremble. [21] For if God did not spare the natural branches, he will not spare you either.
> (Romans 11:17-21)

In contrast to this view of the Christian Church, Paul speaks in Romans of the beginning days of the Gentiles receiving salvation and becoming a part of God's people, the Jews, that placed their faith in Christ as the Messiah. The Gentiles coming to God through Christ were illustrated as "Wild branches" grafted in to the "Natural branches", Israel. Some Natural branches, the segment of Israel that did not receive Jesus as the Messiah were broken off, being replaced by wild branches.

In this grafting-in of the Wild Branches, made up of the nations of the world, a dividing wall of hostility existed during Paul's time between the East and the West. Paul foresaw potential challenges, and declares to the "wild in-grafted Gentile Branches" do not consider yourself to be superior to those other branches.

However following the death of Paul, under Gentile Christianity, the in-grafting process was reversed. Instead of the *Wild Gentile Branches* being grafted in to the *Natural Branch,* the *Natural Branch* (the Hebrew people) were to be grafted in to Gentile Christianity to be a part of God's people, and to renounce their past.

With Islam reflecting the cultural practices of the Jerusalem church, it is this theology which Islam, and the Messenger of Islam, resisted from its beginnings. According to Muhammad, Rome was suppressive towards the East, and theology was used as an instrument to support that. At the time of Muhammad, Muslims had a positive view towards the Torah, which was quite different to the Christian church at the time. For Christians, the Torah represented the past, something that was to be rejected.

However the function of the Torah was never intended to be associated with *becoming God's people*; its instruction was regarding how to *function as God's people.* The Torah was *given* to Israel; to a people who were already undeservedly God's people. The Torah was to help 3 million people to be transformed from refugees in a desert, to a nation that was seen as the most blessed people on earth!

During the beginning years of the Gentiles being grafted in to believing Israel, religious Jews called for obedience to the Torah to become a requirement of Gentiles becoming God's people. God's undeserved grace of receiving a people for himself had been rejected! The function of the Torah had been turned upside down, and Paul confronted this with vigour. The issue was not the Torah, it was how it was being used. Paul said to Timothy:

> *We know that the law is good if one uses it*
> *properly.*
> *(1 Tim 1:8)*

The rise of Islam challenged the replacement theology of Gentile Christianity. Islam reflected more of the Hebrew culture of the

Jerusalem church, as well as the various streams of the Eastern Church that were head-quartered in Antioch. The common practices and beliefs of Islam and Judaism are many, amongst them being:

- Islam and Judaism both have a prescribed amount of prayers per day (5 for Muslims and 3 for Jews).
- Islam and Judaism both have prescribed fasting days (no eating, drinking, or marital relations).
- Islam and Judaism both have a prescribed amount of Zakat (Tithes).
- Islam and Judaism both have a specific direction (*Qiblah*) for prayer; Mecca and Jerusalem (Islam initially facing Jerusalem).
- Islam and Judaism both have a pilgrimage.
- Islam and Judaism practice dietary laws.
- Islam and Judaism both encourage the growing of the beard.
- Islam and Judaism both outlaw usury or interest.
- Islam and Judaism both run by the lunar calendar.
- Islam and Judaism both have a complete system of law that covers economic, criminal, and civil law, and have divine punishments.
- Islam and Judaism both greet each other with the greetings of peace (Assalamu Alaikum = Shalom Aleichem)
- Islam and Judaism both are not allowed to have a dog as a pet.
- Islam and Judaism both outlaw homosexuality.
- Islam and Judaism both outlaw gambling.
- Islam and Judaism both require eating and drinking with the right hand.

This is just a short list amongst hundreds of other common practices and beliefs. And yet despite Islam reflecting much of Judaism, with Islam recognising Jesus as the Messiah, and the Gospels as divinely inspired, it was to have no part with Judaism.

In the 2nd century, the segment of Jews who rejected Christ as the Messiah took the final step in parting ways with the Jewish followers of Christ who had their origins from the Jerusalem church. During that time, in 135AD, the Jews had lead a revolt against the Roman Empire, where they reclaimed Jerusalem for a short period of time under the leadership of Simon bar Kokba. This heroic figure in the eyes of the Jews was declared a Messiah, the deliverer of Israel.

The Jewish followers of Christ, totalling many tens of thousands, could not accept the title of "Messiah" for this warrior, and refused to be involved in the revolt. Consequently, the Jewish revolt was crushed, and it was the last effort of the Jews to reclaim Jerusalem from the Roman Empire. The Jewish community blamed the defeat upon the non-supportive followers of Jesus. From that time forward, Jews who recognised Jesus as the Messiah were not welcome as a part of the Jewish community.

When Muhammad accepted the Christian scriptures, he left behind paganism, and embraced the Hebrew orientated practices that were present amongst a number of communities of Arabia. With this adopting of Hebrew practices, Islam was ostracised from the Christian (Catholic) Church. Additionally, with Jesus recognised as the Messiah by the Islamic community, Islam would experience a separation from the Jewish community. Islam would become a separate entity, being an attractive option of allegiance for the millions of Middle Eastern Christians who were not culturally aligned to Western Christianity.

A journey from extremism to love

Chapter 15:
The Law of Love

I t is significant that the heavenly law that was brought by Jesus could be summed up with only one command. This means that if we live under the guidance and leadership of Jesus, there is only one fundamental requirement.

> *The commandments, "You shall not commit adultery," "You shall not murder," "You shall not steal," "You shall not covet," and whatever other command there may be, are summed up in this one command: "Love your neighbour as yourself." Love does no harm to a neighbour. Therefore love is the fulfilment of the law.*
> *(Roman 13:9-10)*

> *For the entire law is fulfilled in keeping this one command: "Love your neighbour as yourself.*
> *(Gal 5:14)*

According to the Jews, in the Old Testament there are 613 commands. Most non-Jews are familiar with the 10 commandments, which are subdivided into many smaller commands. As the Gentile believers were accepted as members of God's people, they had no background and knowledge of these commands. Also, as previously stated, many of these commands related to the forming of a nation when Israel was coming out of Egypt.

Not only that, but Judaism at the time of Jesus was polarized into sects concerning the oral law and traditions, which are said to have come from Moses. Sadducees didn't follow oral law, Pharisees did. Interpretation of the written Torah also divided the Jewish community. Beyond this, there was the issue of the religious elite, who often were acknowledged by Jesus as having the correct interpretation, but were hypocritical in their actions.

With this confusion amongst the Jews during the time of Jesus, Jesus brought a simple law to live by, centred on love. This was the understanding of all the writers of the New Testament, where the entire Torah that they continued to embrace was viewed through the framework of the heavenly law presented by Jesus, which is to love your neighbour as yourself.

This love that was taught by Jesus wasn't an abstract love, but the love that is experienced in a 'first degree' relationship. A first-degree relationship is the closest possible relationship in a family unit, such as brothers, sisters, mothers and fathers. This is evidenced in Paul writing to Timothy:

> *Do not rebuke an older man harshly, but exhort him as if he were your father. Treat younger men as brothers, older women as mothers, and younger women as sisters, with absolute purity.*
> *(1 Tim 5:1-2)*

> When Jesus spoke in *"Who is my mother and who are my brothers,"*
> *(Matthew 12:48)*

> He was not referring to his biological mother and brothers. He said, *"Whoever does the will of my Father is my brother and sister and mother."*

The parable of the Good Samaritan is insightful in answering the question of 'who is my neighbour?' For the Jews, those outside of their ethnic group were considered unclean and impure. The Jews would have thought that their neighbour could only be someone from amongst themselves, but the heavenly law brought by Jesus identified that love was to be directed to neighbours beyond themselves. In fact, this was to be the identifying mark for Jesus' disciples - that people would know that

> "*you are my disciples, if you have loved one another.*"
> *(John 13:35)*

Concerning this heavenly law, the writers of the New Testament spoke with clarity. John wrote, "*If someone says I love God, and he hates his brother, he is a liar.*" This is profound as we meditate on this. In a culture where love for God was reflected by obedience to external religious rituals, the heavenly law which Jesus brought tied love for God intricately with how one treats others.

> *If you really keep the royal law found in Scripture, "Love your neighbour as yourself," you are doing right.*
> *(James 2:8)*

We are to love others as much as we love ourselves! How much do we love ourselves? How hard do you work to earn money? How hard do you study to get to where you are? To what extent do you go so not to cause harm to yourself? If we are honest, we love ourselves with all our mind, heart and soul.

When we realise how much we love ourselves, we realise the challenge of loving God and loving our neighbour to the same degree. The entire Torah is fulfilled in loving your neighbour as yourself. Scripture doesn't just say love your neighbour, or love one another. That would be very vague. It sets a standard of loving one another to the standard of *"as yourself"*. That means that you treat the other person as though the other person were you.I must look at a totally different person with a totally different culture and even a totally different religion, and love that person as myself. What a challenge! This can only be done through God's enabling by His Spirit!

The Law of Christ - Testimony 1:
Love your enemies

I want to tell you how God transformed my understanding about enemies, and how I need to respond to my "enemy". As a Muslim, who is active in spiritual proclamation to the Islamic community based upon the Holy Books according to the Islamic pillar of faith, I am involved in various forms of media.

On a particular day I visited some active members of our media network. These were members who were different to most Muslims, in that they recognised and attempted to live out the message of the New Testament (Injil). When I met them, they introduced me to an Imam with responsibilities for the region who strongly opposed their stance towards the Bible. The Imam challenged them openly, so when I was there I went to visit this Imam. Usually when someone comes from the city to this visit a regional area like this, it's polite to visit the Imam.

When I arrived at his house, he was extremely angry with me. When he knew I was involved with the proclamation of the message that recognised the Bible as true, he screamed at me. I said, "I have come here as your Muslim brother", but he responded by saying, "Don't call me brother! You are not my brother, you are my enemy. You are my enemy because you have led my people in my mosque astray. You have taught them to believe in Holy Books other than the Holy Qur'an."

Within Islam, you become an enemy and a pagan if you bring false teaching. You are an enemy that needs to be cut off from God's people. The Imam drove me away and said, "Leave here before I do something you'll regret." I told him, "I will pray for you and I will not hate you." Following that, I advised the community of faith that this is a good opportunity for us to pray for this Imam, and not treat him as an enemy.

The following month I returned to the Imam's house. I was thinking about what I could bring for him, as a symbol of brotherhood. Before I left, I bought the nicest looking fruit available and brought it to his home. I said, "This is a gift from my family, I want to give this to you as a blessing for you."

Suddenly, he picked up the fruit, and threw it all away. He said with a harsh voice, "I've said to you before that you are not my brother, you are my enemy! Don't have any expectation that with this gift you bring that I will accept you. You remain my enemy."

I left, giving him my blessing and said that I would pray for him, while he screamed out insults as I climbed on my motorbike.

I returned to the community of faith and said, "We really need to pray for this man. Let's even miss some meals when we pray." Next month, I planned to return, but did not know what could I bring him. I knew if I brought fruit again it would probably end up in the gutter. Therefore, I went to a bookshop and I bought the largest and best Qur'an that was available. It was quite expensive. I arrived at the Imam's house with the Qur'an and extended my greetings. As before, he didn't respond to my greeting. There was still anger.

I told him that I was again visiting his area, and said, "I want to give you this Qur'an as a gift." I knew his heart would be filled with a dilemma, because it was not possible for an Imam to throw the Holy Qur'an into the gutter! He received it, although not inviting me inside. He was just silent, and I permitted myself to leave.

The next month, I came back with nothing. He just looked at me silently. I gave my greetings, and he remained silent. The Imam then said, "Why are you so hard-headed with me? I haven't invited you in as a brother, I've driven you away. Why do you keep on coming back? Have I not been clear to you? Or is there something else that's behind your visiting me? I've told you that you are my enemy! Why do you keep coming back? You've brought fruit, and then brought me the *Qur'an* despite me not accepting you as a brother."

I said to the Imam, "Actually there is no ulterior motive in coming to visit you. I have said to you from the beginning that I love you and will pray for you. Those are not just empty words, but that is my commitment." He said in response, "This is strange. I've never heard someone with this sort of approach."

I knew that this was the opportunity to share the truth of the message that was taught by Jesus. I said to him, "What you have seen me do is what I have been teaching the members in your mosque. This is the teaching we live by. Why do we follow this teaching? Because Jesus taught us concerning everyone who considers themselves as our enemy that we are to pray for them and even bless them. Jesus said, if we love those who love us, this is not any different to the pagans. Even the wicked do that. They love those who love them. For us as people of faith, if we do the same thing, there is no difference between us and the wicked. Jesus taught us that if we are people of faith, we are not only to love those who love us, but to love our enemies. This is what you have been observing. I am just doing what I'm told."

The Imam stood silently. His eyes became watery, like he was about to cry. Within Islam, an Imam does not show his own emotion publicly, so I knew this was a significant moment. God was working in his heart. He felt the love taught by Jesus becoming a reality. He said to me, "How can I experience a similar thing? How can I act like you have acted?" I said, "That is not difficult. You receive what has been prepared and taught by Jesus, and you receive his love."

We prayed together, and I asked him to pray himself to God, asking Jesus into his life. From that time, he personally began to experience God's love. There was a big change that began to happen in his life. He previously had a hard heart, but now his heart was being softened. Love can overcome all things; even the hardest of hearts can be softened. This Imam is now faithfully learning about God's love as he studies the New Testament.

From this experience, I have learned something important. God calls us to love Him, and also to love our neighbour. My neighbour means not only those who are good to me, but those who oppose me. So God challenged me to look for enemies, so they can experience the love that was taught by Jesus. My enemy can become my friend.

Hatred as an obstacle for Christ

Within Islam, there are an increasing number of Muslims who are having a positive outlook towards the teachings of Jesus. In fact, we could say that at the core of it, Islam, as well as Christianity, accepts the teachings of Jesus. However, there is an 'allergy' and hatred towards each other. When there is a love for enemies, the true Jesus will be clearly seen. Hatred of Christians by Muslims and of Muslims by Christians creates a dividing wall not just between themselves, but to the figure of Jesus. There is no basis in Islam to reject Jesus except as a result of hatred towards the 'enemy' that aligns themselves with Jesus.

The lack of loving enemies causes Christ to be pushed aside. Loving your enemies is not just a nice thing to do. It allows non-believers to open the door to receive Christ.

Our relationships with fellow man strongly affect our relationship with God. *Sharia* law reflects the Hebrew perspective of Jesus' day, "love your neighbour and hate your enemies." (Matt 5:43) At the birth of *Sharia* Law, the "enemy" was the pagan or non-monotheists of Mecca, not Christians. However today, the enemy of Islam is considered to be Christians.

The heavenly law declared by Jesus was to love your enemies. God causes the sun to shine upon both the wicked and the righteous. God loves the righteous and also those who reject him. Man loves their neighbour and hates those who reject them. Our challenge is to synchronize ourselves with God and love both.

For a Muslim, those outside of Islam are technically their only enemies. When as Muslims we are challenged to love our enemies, what that really is saying is to love those outside of Islam. For Christians who often see Muslims as enemies, we can see where the commands of Jesus need to be outworked.

Can Muslims have a restored view of non-Muslims as family? Can Christians view Muslims as family? This is the challenge of modern Islam, where contrary to the birth of Islam, Christians are seen as the enemy. Jesus teaches to love your enemies. When we love our enemies, we suddenly realise that they are family, and the walls of division will come down as we embrace the person and teaching of Jesus.

The Law of Christ – Testimony 2: A New Heart

I want to speak to you about how I came to know one of my good friends. He was a young person who, at least externally, seemed to be obedient to the traditions of Islam, like *sholat* and fasting. In fact, he said that if he missed one of the 5 prayers of *sholat*, he felt convicted as a sinner.

One thing he spoke to me about personally, was that even though he was obedient in these areas he had a tendency to easily fall in the area of pornography. When he was on the internet, he would easily be tempted to go to a pornographic site and fall into lustful thoughts. All of this took place while visibly (on the surface) he was seen as obedient to Islamic prayer tradition. When he viewed pornography, he felt dirty within his heart and endeavoured with all his strength to change.

The context of his spiritual life was that he had recently committed his heart to God and received Jesus as his master. He came to me and asked for prayer. He asked me, "How can I become free of something like this pornography?" At this time he was a part time employee of the media proclamation team I was a part of, and it was during this time that he confessed that he had fallen into sexual sin physically. Other staff members learned of this, and opposed him strongly because of his actions. They did not want to have him on staff, as the Islamic proclamation Media Company was founded upon biblical values.

He was full of inner turmoil as he was removed from the media team and began to become less enthusiastic about sharing his new faith. After about a month, he telephoned me and spoke about how he understood why he was removed from the media team, and he apologised to me, as I was the media company director. He explained how he had tried to live a holy life and to follow the suggestions of personal devotions from the scriptures, but once he was rejected by his friends, he had begun to feel a failure. I was reminded of the response of Jesus to the adulterous woman. Jesus forgave, but he was very firm - "Go and sin no more." I said to him, "I won't remove you from the media team, but I want to repeat the words of Jesus, "Go and sin no more."

It was as if at that moment he had a revelation of forgiveness. I said to him, "We need to experience the forgiveness from God." He explained that the motivation behind all of his religious tradition was to pay back the price for his sin. It was at this moment that he had a new understanding of God's forgiveness and his obedience in prayer and fasting rituals was not as a means of payment for his fallen state, but as a desire to be in a quiet place with God.

He spoke of feeling tired in the carrying out of religious tradition, because it didn't bear fruit in overcoming his inner struggles. Up until now, he would do the *sholat* as a means of overcoming his sinful state, but it was unsuccessful. Now, he does the *sholat* to come before his God in worship. This young man has now left his sinful past and is a key part of proclaiming the message of the *Injil*, and now is a living testimony about having a personal heart relationship with God. I can see such a big change in his life.

The Law of Christ - Testimony 3: Turn the other cheek

Not long ago my wife coordinated a gathering of young Muslim women. One young lady who attended was married and felt deceived and unloved by her husband. Her husband was preparing to take a second wife! She had a heart that desired revenge towards her husband, because she was carrying the weight of running their household. Her husband did not have any permanent work, and the wife had to supplement their income by working extra jobs labouring in the field and assisting in a health clinic. This was in addition to getting up early in the morning and doing household duties, preparing food for her husband and their children.

She felt she had given her best to her family and her husband. One day, she found out that her husband had a relationship with another woman and had plans for a second marriage. Her husband approached her about these plans. According to Islamic law, this was something permitted to be pursued by the husband. The wife began to be filled with anger and hate and a desire to divorce her husband.

During this time, despite still being in the house, her heart was not there.

A journey from extremism to love

However the community was advising her, based upon Islamic law, that as a wife she needed to support her husband in marrying a second time. She said, "Well, maybe according to Islamic law that is the case, but I can't lie to myself in the way that I feel. I cannot just accept this action." All the community around her was saying the opposite. However, she stood strong against the advice of her friends, and said that she could not support or forgive her husband.

When this woman met with my wife and myself, and began to experience the fellowship of her small group that was based around the teaching that you are "Fearfully and wonderfully made", she experienced the forgiveness of God through Jesus for the first time. One of the fellowship gatherings included discussion about forgiving others. For this lady, her husband was truly her enemy. She began to see that the anger and hatred within her would destroy her.

Although it was a big struggle, she prayed for her husband. She also knew that the women's group did not support her husband taking a second wife. Through the support of the group, she saw how she could be free from revenge, and even love her husband who at this point, she still viewed as her 'enemy'. Previously, she said she prayed that her husband would be hit by a car!

To be fair, as far as I know, there wasn't any sexual relationship between the husband and the second woman. For him, he was simply following something that he thought was permitted by God.

Being free from the desire for revenge caused a big change in the content of the prayers of this wife. She prayed that the plans of her husband would not be realised, and that this plan for a second marriage would not proceed. She prayed in a new way. We advised her not to divorce, but to serve her family the best she could. This was a big challenge; just to look at her husband's face caused emotions to stir within her – he was someone she had grown to despise. What's more, to get up and prepare him breakfast! These feelings continued, but through her prayers she had hope for the future.

For about a month, there was no change, and she began to share with her support group that this idea wasn't working. She saw that there was no change in her husband and began to make plans to leave him. We continued to pray together with her about loving your enemies, in particular, forgiving not so that you can get something, but forgiving no matter what the outcome is. Through this she was able to find new resolve to hope for a solution.

Two months from her initial sharing with the small group, and endeavouring to forgive and serve her husband, she was accepted as a staff member in a hospital. However, not only that, an issue emerged in the other relationship of her husband, and he returned to his wife and asked forgiveness. They are now united together as a happily married husband and wife. What's more, her husband made a commitment never to pursue another woman!

This family lived under an earthly law, but the woman is an example of embracing Christ's law. They are now our close friends. Our prayer is that our actions would reflect that which is taught by Christ, even when things are clearly unfair! In this case, love your enemies and persist in praying for those who persecute you.

Chapter 16:
The World I see on the horizon –
Two brothers united
Farid Ibrahim

The world I see on the horizon is that of two brothers re-united. These brothers had a painful separation thousands of years ago.

Abraham's Farewell to Ishmael
By George Segal

The older and younger brother represents a truth from the Torah. They were born from one father, and different mothers. Ishmael is the older physical brother; Isaac is the older spiritual brother. This is the beginning of a common monotheism together, these two brothers whose descendants were separated. They both embraced the monotheism of their father, Abraham.

Just as the younger brother, Isaac, was given a command - a mandate - that he would seek his older brother who left the tent of Abraham, so also Jesus commanded the descendants of Isaac to seek their older brother, seeking the one who had been driven out of the tent of Abraham long ago to invite him home. (Matt 28:18)

The descendants of Isaac have been given guidance about how to speak to their older brother, and how to express the news that is needed by Ishmael. God has given us a way to speak to our older brother, who was long ago driven out from the family, resulting in a heart that is wounded.

There was an eternal promise that would come through the descendants of Isaac. That promise was given a long time before Ishmael was born. There are a number of important things we need to consider when referring to this promise.

To Ishmael:

> *And as for Ishmael, I have heard thee: Behold, I have blessed him, and will make him fruitful, and will multiply him exceedingly; twelve princes shall he beget, and I will make him a great nation.*
> *(Gen 17:20)*

To Isaac:

> *Stay in this land for a while, and I will be with you and will bless you. For to you and your descendants I will give all these lands and will confirm the oath I swore to your father Abraham. I will make your descendants as numerous as the stars in the sky and will give them all these lands, and through your offspring all nations on earth will be blessed.*
> *(Gen 26: 3 - 4)*

Firstly the promise of descendants was a common promise given to the two brothers. Secondly, the promise of blessing would be given to the two sons, Ishmael and Isaac. And finally, the eternal promise was given to the descendants of Isaac only, that through Abraham's seed, that is Christ, all the nations will be blessed. The descendants of Isaac are responsible to tell their older brother about this promise.

*And through your offspring all nations on earth
will be blessed, because you have obeyed me."
(Gen 22:18)*

*The promises were spoken to Abraham and to
his seed. Scripture does not say "and to seeds,"
meaning many people, but "and to your seed,"
meaning one person, who is Christ.
(Gal 3:16)*

If the descendants of Ishmael do not hear about the promise that
was given through their younger brother, they will simply be
waiting; waiting for Isaac's descendants to speak about the eternal
promise which the younger brother inherited.

The guidelines for sharing this eternal promise with the older
brother are clear. In *1 Peter*, there are three things prescribed for
talking to your older brother. That is, to speak with a pure heart,
speak with respect, and speak with humility. That is how we are
to speak to our older brother.

The younger brother has been equipped with authority to meet
with the older brother. However there is a wound between the
two. The younger brother views the older brother as illegitimate
and looks upon Ishmael with negativity. The character of the
younger needs to be conformed to the character of Christ. The
younger is to come with a new spirit, an approach that softens the
heart of his older brother. In light of this, Isaacs' descendants do
not need to fear meeting with his older brother, as love overcomes
fear.

Jesus said, "For God so loved the world!" He didn't say, "For God
so loved the descendants of Isaac", but the whole world, and that
includes the descendants of the *two* brothers. The older brother
needs to be restored to the tent of Abraham! However it will
require patience. Usually, the older brother speaks more. They
like to be the teacher. In Eastern culture, the older brother usually

gets angry with the younger if he is not living according to his expectations. We need to be patient with the older brother, who has experienced bitterness for a long time. It's our older brother who was driven out of the tent. We need to pray for our older brother so that he can come home.

Our approach can not be to debate with our older brother, but rather to be willing to listen, even though he is upset. For me personally, in leading the descendants of Ishmael to the eternal promise, I constantly allow the older brother to talk a lot, so that I know how to respond. If I don't know anything about my older brother, I don't know how to respond.

This is the historical truth of the two brothers. For Jesus, the older brother was to be an object of love because he was driven out of the tent of Abraham, and it's the responsibility of the younger brother to bring him home. The older brother is emotional; there will be a major conflict if the younger brother responds with the same emotion. This is one of the foundations for me in bringing the eternal promise to the descendants of Ishmael, understanding the character of the two brothers.

The future I see on the horizon is the two brothers being re-united together! It will require humility. Paul tells us of the simple truth of a reunited family:

> If you belong to Christ, then you are Abraham's
> seed, and heirs according to the promise.
> (Gal 3: 29)

There are so many religious traditions accumulated by Isaac's descendants, both cultural and theological, that are seen by the younger brother as requirements to receive Ishmael back into the tent of Abraham. However receiving Ishmael back does not need to be complicated. Ishmael needs to see Christ as the expression of God's love, and Ishmael needs to see that love in a younger brother welcoming him home.

The World I see on the horizon
Daniel Roberts

The reuniting of the two brothers is the future we dream of together. However as a Christian, it will require leaving behind baggage that has been accumulated over many centuries.

As a Christian from the West, I have been born into:

- An attitude concerning Muhammad and Islam that is primarily based upon Islam being a political enemy, and that attitude has remained with us until this day.
- An attitude that the Christian religion is the only path to salvation. However historically, Christianity has been the religion under the rulership of Rome. As you can be read in Appendix 1, being a part of God's people is beyond this.
- An attitude towards Eastern culture of "replacement theology". As we see people doing the *Sholat* and other Hebrew practices, a common attitude is that these practices have been replaced by the *'freedom of Western Christianity.'* However the culture of Islam is largely the culture of the *'Natural Branches,'* God's people of the Old Testament.

Although much has changed in Christianity compared to the era of Muhammad, Islam is generally unaware of these changes, and has an ongoing 7th Century understanding of Christianity as a vehicle to extend the Western World's Political Empire.

The future of the two brothers reuniting partly depends upon these attitudes being shaken off. Thankfully today, there is increasing movement in the direction of the two brothers being reunited. What was seemingly impossible in the past has become possible for the future - a future where there is a breaking down of the dividing wall of hostility.

The World I see on the Horizon
Usman Kadir

Following my heart transformation, my responsibilities continued as an Imam, as an educator, and as a mentor for *Madrassah's*. When I had previously functioned in these roles, I was harsh in regards to obedience to *Sharia* law. However, after my heart transformation, my message began to change.

At first this was difficult, but as I continued as a Friday preacher, I realised God wanted a new type of preacher that brought a new spirit to Islam. I recognised that the function of the *Qur'an* was to point toward the former revelation, that being the Bible. My task is now to bring my Muslim brothers and sisters back to the message of our messenger, that is, to accept and embrace that which is foreign to us - the Hebrew prophets, the Hebrew Bible, and the Hebrew Messiah. This is the reformed Islam of the future, following in the footsteps of its founder.

The change that has taken place in my life is profound. I think there is a simple event that really demonstrates this change. My family and I regularly catch a public bus. Even in regards to this simple task of climbing into public transport, under *Sharia* law there was a particular process to this. The passengers, even though they were fellow Muslims, would move away from me out of fear. I remember my wife saying to me once, "Everyone is scared of us wherever we go!" There was a strong concept that I was someone to be feared. I don't remember ever smiling.

After my transformation, comments were being circulated about how friendly the new religious leader was (me), and how warm his smile was. I asked them one day, "Why didn't you like sitting next to me before?"

I told them, "That behaviour was what I was taught according to the modern interpretation of *Sharia*. That was how anyone

A journey from extremism to love

following *Sharia* Law is supposed to act. Why haven't you asked me what kind of law I am following now?" Whatever it was they perceived I had embraced, they were pleased I was following it! Now they sit close to their smiling Imam on public transport! They saw within me a new law, a law of love and compassion, the law of Christ.

The transformation that I experienced is not intended to remain as just my own story. My story has now been reproduced in the lives of thousands of other Muslims. They have experienced a new heart. We need to welcome a new day!

My dream is that a new generation of Muslim preachers will bring a message of a merciful and compassionate God who sent Jesus as the expression of His mercy and love. We have a global vision, dreaming to fly like eagles, not restricted by the traditional restraints of *Sharia*. Instead of *Sharia* Law, we can now dream with a yoke that is light and easy!

I have a cry in my heart that comes as a result of my years of living under *Sharia*. It is for my fellow Muslims NOT to leave their people or their religious identity for another, but for them to experience a transformation of love found in Christ.

As a child in my village, I looked across the river and saw a Christian village that did not live according to the traditions of Islam, and I used to wonder how I could enjoy playing their games. At that time, the Christian kids and I were all innocent youth playing in the river. Later as a teenager I started wondering how they could become like us, and embrace Islam? At the same time, the Christians on the opposite side of the river were asking the same question, "How they could become like us, and become Christians?"

Sometimes life's journey brings us in a full circle. After departing my small home town as a 15 year old with no idea of the journey that lay ahead, decades later I sat in a room with a western man whose name sounded familiar. As we began to talk, I realised this western man was from the missionary family across the other side of the river in my childhood.

Thirty five years later here we were, me an Imam, he a Christian worker. However there was no longer a chasm that divided us, and we embraced as brothers. Many years ago he had learnt to welcome Ishmael back as his brother, and accept his differences. We both recognised Christ as the Word from God for mankind, and with that we had a common father in Abraham.

The following 2 Appendices provide a historical background of Islam. The 1ˢᵗ Appendix relates to the development of the Jewish church which would have a significant influence upon Islam. The 2ⁿᵈ Appendix focuses on the key individual who is the link between the Jewish Church and Muhammad.

Appendix 1:
Do not call anyone impure or unclean...

T wo thousand years ago, Peter experienced a dilemma. He, being a Jew, believed together with the church that salvation through Jesus their Messiah was only for Jews. One religion, Judaism, was the path for salvation for those following the Christ. This was not the view of an isolated few. It was the view of one of the disciples closest to Jesus, Peter. It was the view of the Jerusalem church.

This was the context of the church, when Peter entered a house of someone with whom he thought he was not supposed to associate – Gentile, Cornelius:

He said to them:
> *"You are well aware that it is against our law for a Jew to associate with or visit a Gentile. But God has shown me that I should not call anyone impure or unclean."*
> *(Acts 10:28)*

> *Then Peter began to speak: "I now realize how true it is that God does not show favouritism."*
> *(Acts 10:34)*

> *The circumcised believers who had come with Peter were astonished that the gift of the Holy Spirit had been poured out even on Gentiles.*
> *(Acts 10:45)*

> When they heard this, they had no further
> objections and praised God, saying, "So
> then, even to Gentiles God has granted
> repentance that leads to life."
> *(Acts 11:18)*

God was challenging the paradigm of the church! *But God has shown me that I should not call anyone impure or unclean* was how Peter viewed Non-Jewish people, whether ourselves - or Muslims. This was not about God challenging the church over the food they ate! Despite the vision being related to food, the application was intended to challenge the way God's people viewed other peoples.

The message becomes increasingly clear with a study of the Greek words for impure and unclean. Peter viewed Gentiles as intrinsically unclean (Greek: *Akathartos*), meaning there was no hope of them being purified. In the view of Peter and the church, Gentiles were born *Akathartos* (Unclean: Acts 10:28). No matter what ceremonial processes they went through, they would be required to no longer be a Gentile to be considered clean.

In addition to this, the word "impure" in Acts 10:28 (Greek: *Koinos*) meant being intrinsically clean, but still contaminated by its surroundings. And so the common belief of the church was that Gentiles were both *Akathartos* for simply being Gentiles, and *Koinos* for being in contact with unclean foods and pagan gods.

However in Acts 10, God revealed to Peter that not only were Gentiles intrinsically clean, but also that, despite Gentiles living in contact with gods and unclean foods, they were not to be called *Koinos* (impure).

God revealed his heart to Peter, that God does not show favouritism with any particular religious or ethnic group. (Acts 10:34) On the one hand there were the Jews, a people with a history of thousands of years, a people called for a special purpose, with the God of Abraham, Isaac and Jacob having a covenant with them to bear witness to His Name. On the other hand, other peoples, the Gentiles, who were known as a people who worshipped idols and ate food offered to idols, were referred to as "dogs".[30]

God reveals to Peter, that He shows no favouritism. In regards to salvation, even the religion of Peter, Judaism, has no benefit in God's eyes. This is evidenced by the Holy Spirit being poured out upon non-Jews, with the Jewish church that was present being astonished!

Paul would say later,

> There is neither Jew nor Gentile, neither slave nor free, nor is there male and female, for you are all one in Christ Jesus.
> *(Galatians 3:28)*

In Christ, there is no advantage with gender (male or female), no advantage with position (slave or free), and no advantage with religion and race (Jew or Gentile). In Cornelius and his household

Peter found a spiritual family he never knew he had!

> *The apostles and the believers throughout Judea heard that the Gentiles also had received the word of God. So when Peter went up to Jerusalem, the circumcised believers criticized him and said, "You went into the house of uncircumcised men and ate with them."*
> *Starting from the beginning, Peter told them the whole story.*
> *(Acts 11:1-4)*

---

[30] *Matt 15:26*: Jesus' reference to the Gentiles as "dogs" was the traditional name of Jews in referring to "The Nations." However Jesus left tradition in recognising the faith of a Gentile.

After this experience, word quickly spread amongst the church that the Gospel message was accepted by Non-Jews. Peter returned to Jerusalem, being criticized for his actions by the church: "You entered in to an unclean place! Peter, we would agree with you converting them to Judaism to follow our Messiah, Jesus, but having them remain there and say they are one with us?

But Peter began to tell the story....

> When they heard this, they had no further objections and praised God, saying, "So then, even to Gentiles God has granted repentance that leads to life."
> *(Acts 11:18)*

And so it was, for you and me as Gentile believers, this is the beginning of our journey. We were welcomed as a part of a spiritual family. This discussion and approval of Peter's actions in the face of criticism could have taken place very quickly; however it would have eternal consequences for us, being welcomed as family members. A spiritual family that was intended to be not bound together by a particular gender (male or female), a particular status (slave or free), or even a particular religious or racial group (Jew or Gentile).

During the following years, despite generally the Jewish church continuing in the view that religious allegiance would be determined by whether someone could be a part of God's family through Christ, some followed the example of Peter. And this was the beginning of an explosion of this new type of "family member", the Gentile!

> *The disciples were called Christians first at Antioch.*
> *(Acts 11:26)*

It was at this time that these new family members, being "grafted in to the olive tree[31]", began to be called a label. "Christian!"[32] It may have begun with a few who sought to make fun of them. They could have been local Non-believing Jews. Those mocking them could have felt insulted that the "Pagans" were viewing themselves as a part of "God's people" through the death of a Jew called Jesus.

Often those being called a particular name take it on themselves and the name remains. And so these new family members began to welcome their own distinct name, Christian. Later this would have bigger implications…..

> Then some of the believers who belonged to the party of the Pharisees stood up and said, "The Gentiles must be circumcised and required to keep the law of Moses."
> (Acts 15:5)

> "It is my judgment, therefore, that we should not make it difficult for the Gentiles who are turning to God."
> (Acts 15:19)

> Then they said to Paul: "You see, brother, how many thousands of Jews have believed, and all of them are zealous for the law.
> (Acts 21:20)

The older members of God's family, the Christ-following Jewish community, were zealous for the law! James, the brother of Jesus,

---

[31] Romans 11:17

[32] The 3 verses in the Bible for the word "Christian" (Greek: Christianos) are in Acts 11:26; Acts 26:28 and 1 Peter 4:16. There is no passage where Christs followers are using the term "Christian" in reference to themselves.

made yet another decision which had a dramatic impact upon us as Gentile Christians. Gentiles were not to carry the burden of the laws of the Jews for salvation, except *to abstain from food polluted by idols, from sexual immorality, from the meat of strangled animals and from blood,*[33] and the new family members rejoiced!

> After Gentile Christians become recognised as a legitimate part of the family
> *(Acts 11:18)*
>
> after the customs of one family member, the Jews, are not imposed upon others
> *(Acts 15:19)*
>
> Paul has some critical advice for the newest members of God's family....
>
> I am talking to you Gentiles. Do not consider yourself to be superior to those other branches. If you do, consider this: You do not support the root, but the root supports you.
> *(Romans 11:13)*

Paul says, *Remember from where you came! You are the new family members; don't become arrogant because of this fact. We are the fruit of Paul's vision he saw, God's family made up of Jews and Gentiles, a great multitude.*

Paul was aggressive in confronting a sense of superiority amongst "Family members". To the older family members of the circumcision, he was ruthless if they imposed their law as a requirement of salvation upon Gentiles, in addition to their faith in Christ.

---

[33] *Acts 15: 20*

As for the Jews, Paul also made a commitment so that he would not encourage any of his fellow Jews who confessed Jesus as the Christ to leave their customs, or their religion.

> *Then they said to Paul: "You see, brother, how many thousands of Jews have believed, and all of them are zealous for the law.*
>
> *They have been informed that you teach all the Jews who live among the Gentiles to turn away from Moses, telling them not to circumcise their children or live according to our customs.*
>
> *What shall we do?*
>
> *Take these men, join in their purification rites and pay their expenses, so that they can have their heads shaved. Then everyone will know there is no truth in these reports about you, but that you yourself are living in obedience to the law*
>
> *The next day Paul took the men and purified himself along with them.*
>
> *(Acts 20:20-26)*

One in Christ, despite different genders, different status and different religions!

As the earliest family members, the Jewish church began to suffer. From the time of Paul, division and suspicion grew between Jew and Gentile. The Jerusalem church was suspicious of Paul. His Jewish community suspected him of encouraging Jews to leave the teachings of Moses. Paul strongly denied it, taking a vow in the temple as evidence that he had never done such a thing!!

Even during the era of the Apostles, the *new family* was experiencing trouble. For many Jews, Paul was a traitor.

However, that was only half of the problem.

> *These are the only Jews among my co-workers for the kingdom of God, and they have proved a comfort to me.*
> *(Colossians 4:11)*

The Gentile church grew. Initially the apostolic team were only Jews; however, within 20 years, the apostolic team together with Paul were all Gentiles except for a couple of Jews. Certainly the family was becoming as John visualised in the book of Revelation:

> *After this I looked, and there before me was a great multitude that no one could count, from every nation, tribe, people and language, standing before the throne and before the Lamb. They were wearing white robes and were holding palm branches in their hands.*
> *(Rev. 7:9)*

By now there was true diversity. However, instead of following Peter's vision - *that God shows no favouritism* - the Gentile Church, who were increasingly known as "Christians", began to transition into the **only members of the family.** Instead of an acceptance of diversity – in which, as Paul stated, "the God of the Jews was the God of the Gentiles"[34] - an institution evolved that was suspicious of anything outside of its structure.

With nearly 2,000 years of History, it is easy to paint any sort of picture of Christianity: either one of bringing blessing, or one of bringing turmoil. I am committed to and positive about the church! We are living in exciting times where I am sure the stories

---

[34] *Romans 3:29*

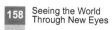

and concepts in this book would not have been acceptable in the past. However there are parts of Church History that have contributed to where we are today. As we look at the developments after the life of the Apostles, it seems clear that rapidly the Gentile church became the *only church*, and that the Gentile church began to view its structure as the only path of salvation.

Within 100 years after Paul, Justin Martyr declared that the scriptures that previously were from Israel were now under the ownership of Christians,[35] and stated that the Jews should "rightly suffer," for they had "slain the Just One".

Approximately 150 years after Paul, the powerful Bishop of Carthage in the third century concluded that there was no salvation outside the institution of the church, the Gentile church, which was to be subject to the control of the bishop.[36] The motivation was to eliminate heresy. It eliminated something else: the diversity of the family that John saw in the book of Revelation.

About 275 years after Paul, the Gentile church compiled the Nicene Creed. Those who did not commit to it were said to have no part in the church. And just over 300 years after Paul, the Gentile church was integrated with the Roman Empire; individuals who did not adhere to the creed created in Constantinople were not just heretics within the church, but criminals of the state. Books that contradicted the doctrine of the state were to be burned.[37]

Paul visualised a family that was to be united despite differences in gender, position and religious allegiances. Rather than being

---

[35] *Justine Martyr, Dialogue with Trypho*

[36] *Cyprian's letter (Epistle LXXII, 21)*

[37] *Non-compliance to the Nicea Creed resulted in an "Anathema" declared upon the individual. The term 'anathema' means a form of extreme religious sanction beyond excommunication, known as major excommunication. Notice is sent in writing to the priests and neighbouring bishops of the name of the one who has been thus excommunicated and the cause of his excommunication, in order that they may have no communication with him, and is delivered to Satan and his angels.*

new family members accepted into the family, we **are** the family. Many may say that Christianity is not a religion for them, but a relationship with Christ. However at the same moment we are seriously sceptical of the validity of salvation of someone who is a part of another religious community, outside of "Christianity".

Let us re-look at Peter's experiences and be honest; we are struggling through Peter's paradigm! Peter was representing the "Chosen Nation", Israel, and the people he was referring to, the Gentiles, were known as idol worshipers. Placing ourselves in Peter's position, as a part of the Christian church, struggling to learn from Peter's experience when viewing the descendants of Ishmael:

> *But God has shown me that I should not call*
> *anyone impure or unclean*
> *(Acts 10:28) .*

We can identify with Peter. The paradigm of a Christian is often that a Muslim is spiritually unclean. Do we view Muslims as intrinsically unclean (*Akathartos*), holding the view that as long as a person remains a Muslim, they are not a disciple of Christ? Or do we view a Muslim as impure (*Koinos*), meaning that they are contaminated by remaining in their surroundings?

> *"I now realize how true it is that God does not*
> *show favouritism."*
> *(Acts 10:34)*

God accepts Christians; it is they who go to heaven, don't they? Well, God has a far greater plan. He shows no favouritism. Despite our negative attitudes, His grace is for all peoples.

> *Is the same Holy Spirit poured out upon "even"*
> *those who have put their faith in Christ yet*
> *remain identified as Muslims? Ultimately the*

*repentance granted to Muslims comes back to
one thing. Do we believe that the same Holy
Spirit that leads us is capable of leading the
Muslim through daily life? Or do we remove the
person from a Muslim background to the
"safety" of Gentile Christianity? So if God has
given Muslims the same gift of the Holy Spirit as
he has given us, who am I to think that I could
oppose God?*
(Acts 11:17)

Allowing Muslims who embrace God's word to remain outside of
a "recognisably traditional Christianity" will attract criticism!
That also happened 2000 years ago when the Jews saw that only
they were God's people and that Gentile were unclean. We simply
have a choice. Do we embrace the Word of God revealed to Peter,
which breaks down ethnic pride and says "Do not call any man
impure or unclean?"

At this point, I should mention about the Jewish Church, because
ultimately it was the Jewish church which had a significant
influence during the earliest days of Islam. The Gentile church
experienced a total separation - possibly within 100 years - from
the Jewish church. The reasons for the Christian Gentile church
separating are complex, including that of the church taking a stand
on theological issues.[38]

However in some ways, this would seem to be an escape from
other underlying issues. We discern throughout the 2nd to 4th
centuries an attitude of the church towards those Jewish believers
that went beyond theological. Semitic peoples were to renounce
their customs, culture, and who they were as people. Many official
statements of the church could be used to indicate this. The
following is an example of the attitude embraced by much of the
church during this period…

---

[38] *Refer to page   concerning the "Hebrew Mind and Greek Mind" for more clarity about
the roots of this division.*

If any clergyman or layman shall enter into a synagogue of Jews or heretics to pray, let the former be deposed and let the latter be excommunicated.[39]

From Jesus growing up celebrating Jewish Festivals annually (Luke 2), and reading the scrolls in the synagogue, to Paul and the apostles following their custom of synagogue attendance, there seems to be a major shift from the picture of unity between the Semitic and Gentile disciples in scripture to the statement above.

As was his custom, Paul went into the synagogue.
(Acts 17:2)

Someone coming into the Gentile Christian church that came from a Jewish background was required to renounce all, as the following official church statement explains:

I renounce all customs, rites, legalisms, unleavened breads and sacrifice of lambs of the Hebrews, and all the other feasts of the Hebrews, sacrifices, prayers, aspersions, purifications, sanctifications, and propitiations, and fasts, and new moons, and Sabbaths, and superstitions, and hymns and chants and observances and synagogues, and the food and drink of the Hebrew; in one word, I renounce absolutely everything Jewish.[40]

The vision from God to Peter to not call any man unclean or impure seems to have been long forgotten. Placing these renunciations beside the customs of the Apostles, something has dramatically changed:

---

[39] *CATHOLIC ENCYCLOPEDIA: Apostolic Canons*
[40] ^ Parks, James (1974), *The Conflict of The Church and The Synagogue*, New York: Atheneum, pp. 397–98.

*Take these men, join in their purification rites
and pay their expenses, so that they can have
their heads shaved. Then everyone will know
there is no truth in these reports about you, but
that you yourself are living in obedience to the
law.* [26] *The next day Paul took the men and
purified himself along with them.*

(Acts 21:24, 26)

Diversity in the spiritual family, where Jew and Greek both existed, by this time had started to fade away.

With the Gentile church being the "One true church", there was an opposition to literature that varied from the church's doctrine, including the burning of literature that was sympathetic with Jewish practices. Partly due to this, we have limited information about the history of the Jewish church.

What we do know is that the Jerusalem church was led by James, the brother of Jesus, for close to 20 years. He was considered a man of great wisdom, gaining the name "James the Just." Ironically we Christians are accepted as a part of God's family without the requirement of salvation through following the Jewish practices, because of the strong stance of James in Acts 15.

Following the martyrdom of the disciples, the destruction of Jerusalem occurred where the Jewish church was scattered to the hills of Judea. There is some evidence that the Jewish church continued to be led until the early 2nd Century by the relatives of Jesus himself,[41] including the grandchildren of Jude, Jesus' 3rd brother[42] and the writer of a New Testament letter.

The Jewish church, scattered after the destruction of Jerusalem, lived in relative poverty compared to the Gentile church.

---

[41] *The History of Jewish Christianity, Hugh Schonfield, 1936*
[42] *Mark 6:3*

There is a deep tragedy in the end of the once powerful and respected Church of the Apostles. No sudden and merciful extinction was granted to the ancient communities of Jewish Believers; but slow decay set in which in the course of time reduced their number to a few fragmentary groups who had almost forgotten their own origin.[43]

At least in part, this sad history is the result of the rejecting of God's plan for cultural and religious diversity amongst His people.

With the rise of Islam, the real work of Jewish believers in the East had (in a sense) finished. It had left in possession at least a faith in which the Unity of God was a fundamental principle and in which Jesus was recognized as *the Messiah promised in the Old Testament.*"[44]

In one sense, the Jewish Church that was founded by the 12 Apostles in the Jerusalem Church did not cease to exist in the period shortly prior to Muhammad. Instead the DNA of the Jerusalem Church continued to exist amongst millions of Christians throughout the Middle East. This was the "Hebrew orientated church". This is the Church to which the Islam which Muhammad brought, not the Islam of today, would be closely linked.

We need to put aside the traditional Christian attitudes, and remember that we are speaking of a different Islam that we may have been taught. If you are like the average Christian, when you hear these topics, it is likely that you would have been at least influenced with the view that "Islam promotes violence" or that the religion of Islam is "spiritually evil."[45] The challenge is for us to remember Peter's revelation: "Do not call anyone unclean or impure." Remember, those represented by our brothers are a part of our family that was revealed to John, a great multitude of diversity![46]

---

[43] *The History of Jewish Christianity, Hugh Schonfield, 1936*
[44] *The History of Jewish Christianity, Hugh Schonfield, 1936*
[45] *http://www.christianpost.com/news/survey-protestant-pastors-view-islam-with-suspicion-44871/*
[46] *Rev 7:9*

Appendix 2:
Waraqa Bin Nauful: The Missing Link

In the following description of the overlooked mentor figure of the Messenger of Islam, Waraqa Bin Nauful, I have taken the approach of seeking to build a bridge, rather than creating further walls of division. over some aspects that cannot be determined with certainty.

The life calling of Waraqa Bin Nauful

> *"The Monk Waraqa wrote the Arabic Book. He wrote from the Hebrew Gospel."*
> *(Al-Bukhari)*

As Muhammad's life-time tutor and mentor, *Nasoro* (Nazarene) Priest *Waraqa Bin Nauful*, faithfully translated the Hebrew version of Matthew into Arabic until he had reached his 100th year, it was the translating of a Gospel that had been recognised by the Nazarenes since the apostolic era.

Despite the descendants of the Jerusalem Church being distanced by the "Official Church", the Church Fathers recognised the Nazarenes as holding devoutly to the Hebrew Gospel of Matthew throughout the centuries leading up to the era of *Waraqa Bin Nauful*.

The early Church Father, Irenaeus, in the early 2nd century declared that the Hebrew Gospel of Matthew had been written during the lifetime of Peter and Paul in the AD50's:

"Matthew also issued a written Gospel among the Hebrews in their own dialect while Peter and Paul were preaching the gospel at Rome and founding the church there." (Irenaeus, Against Heresies, Book III)

Some 250 years later Epiphanius (310-403 AD), Bishop of Salamis, declared the following:

"The Nazarenes maintained Matthew's Gospel in the Hebrew as it was originally written. But these sectarians... did not call themselves Christians – but Nazoreans [i.e., 'Nazarenes'] who confess that Christ Jesus is the Son of God, but all of whose customs are in accordance with the Law.... They use not only the New Testament but the Old Testament as well, as the Jews do. (Epiphanius, The Panarion of Epiphanius of Salamis)

Some decades after Epiphanius, Jerome (342 AD–420 AD) was requested by Pope Damasus in 382 AD to produce a new standard Latin version of the Bible. Jerome stated that Matthew wrote his gospel originally in Hebrew, and it was later translated into Greek. Jerome was clear that he believed the Hebrew Gospel preserved by the Nazarenes kept in a Library of Caesarea was the authentic original. Jerome makes no charge of unorthodoxy against the Hebrew version of Matthew, and quotes the Hebrew Gospel According to Matthew with great respect and admiration.

Being ostracised by the Christian Church as well as Judaism, the Nazarenes continued the Hebrew tradition of protecting the scriptures, transferring it from generation to generation, whilst the Christian Church canonised the four Greek Gospels.

Based upon quotations of the Hebrew Gospel of Matthew from the Church Fathers, the content had minimal variations to the Greek version of Matthew held by the Catholic Church. The Jewish followers of the Way, the Nazarenes, were scattered throughout the region bringing copies of the Hebrew Gospel of Matthew to locations that became their new homeland. Networks of Nazarenes resided in Arabia, with one well respected leader and Priest of the Nazarenes, Waraqa Bin Nauful, living in the pagan city of Mecca, committed to translating the Hebrew Gospel of Matthew so to be understood by his people.

A journey from extremism to love

The Background of Waraqa Bin Nauful

An important starting point in understanding Waraqa Bin Nauful is that Waraqa, Muhammad, and his wife Khadijah all being cousins of the *Quraysh* tribe, were associated with the Nazarenes, referred to in the *Qur'an* as *Nasara* (2:62, 5:18). This community were said to be the continuation of the early Jewish followers of Jesus, identified in Acts 24:5.

From the earliest days, the Nazarenes had carried a pain concerning the Apostle Paul. In Acts 21:20, the Jerusalem Church had been wrongly informed that the Apostle Paul taught Jews who live amongst Gentiles to turn away from Moses. As a result, from the time shortly after Paul, up until the time of Waraqa, the Nazarenes never recognised the writings of Paul, instead clinging to the Hebrew version of Matthew.

Throughout Arabia, there were numerous communities of Nazarenes. According to Arab literature, the Roman Church at one stage sided with the pagans of Arabia to defeat two of the Nazarene clans in the region. (Azzi, 2005)

Prior to embracing the Nazarenes who recognized Jesus as the Messiah, Waraqa belonged to the religion of Moses, following its devout monotheism. This is the foundation for the emphasis of the *Qur'an*, which repeatedly calls people to the Torah and the Gospel.

> *People of the Book, you have no foundation*
> *unless you uphold the Torah (of Moses) and*
> *the Gospel and what was revealed to you by*
> *your Lord.*
> *(QS 5:68)*

This emphasis upon scripture was foundational to the ministry of Waraqa. As a Nazarene, this understanding of Jesus the Christ was less theological and developed than many of the neighbouring

Christians. The faith of Waraqa was in a context of creedal wars that had divided the church within the region.

The Nazarene community entered Mecca at least four generations earlier. Islam until this day generally only knows one line of Muhammad's genealogy, with the other line being rich in Nazarene tradition. The emphasis is upon pre-Islamic paganism and polytheism, with Muhammad bringing the pagan community of Mecca back to the God of Abraham. There is truth to this; however, it covers over a great missing link of Muhammad to the Nazarene community, which traces its roots back to the Jerusalem church.

The Nazarene community was deeply integrated with the Jewish belief system. However, it had no central hierarchy, but simply recognising the 12 apostles as their first community of faith. The Nazarene community itself was divided by various beliefs. For Waraqa and Muhammad, Jesus was born of a virgin and being himself the very Word of God.

> Truly the Messiah, Jesus son of Mary is Gods
> Messenger and His Word.
> (QS 4:171)

Many other Nazarene communities did not hold to these beliefs. The *Qur'an* confronts the division of the Nazarene communities when it says, *"They are divided into sects."* (QS 30:32) For Muhammad, his calling was to bring unity amongst these communities.

The Nazarene community of Mecca had access to the Hebrew Gospel, with Waraqa devoting much time translating it into Arabic. Within the *Qur'an*, the Gospel is never presented in plural form, i.e. "Gospels". The single Gospel of the Qur'an appears to be the Hebrew Gospel of Matthew. In Surah 3:3, the Qur'an reveals the Gospel is God's message through Jesus, the son of Mary.

In a sense, the *Qur'an* is a promotion of the only Gospel known to the Nazarene community in Mecca. Waraqa Bin Nauful was the leader of this church in Mecca, having responsibilities for instruction and interpretation of Scripture. He had the responsibility to explain to his people spiritual matters in which they were largely ignorant. This led him to translate the Hebrew Gospel of Matthew, so that it could be understood in a meaningful way by the Meccan community.

One of the tasks of Waraqa as the local priest was to mentor and equip a young man by the name of Muhammed. Waraqa was instrumental in facilitating the marriage to Muhammad's wife, Khadijah. He introduced his practice of fasting and prayer to in the caves of Mount Hara. Muhammad and Waraqa were on a life journey together to direct the Arabian people to the Gospel they knew. A *Hadith* that is recognized by Muslims today states:

> *Since Waraqa's death, revelation dried up.*
> *(Al-Bukhari, Sahih Vol.1, p38)*

This emphasizes the vital role that Waraqa had in the mission of Muhammad. He was the wise guide who Muhammad looked to for advice. Waraqa was a hundred years old at the time of his death, with Muhammad being 44 years old.

Historians are divided concerning the faith of Waraqa at his death. Did he die as a Muslim or as a Nazarene? This reflects a foundational misunderstanding of Muhammad's mission. Islam was a state of the heart that pagans in Arabia needed to embrace. It was not a competing religious allegiance to Waraqa. In fact, some Islamic historians wish that Waraqa was condemned in eternity for not embracing Islam. However, Muhammad says,

> *"I saw him in the centre of paradise. He was*
> *wrapped in a white shroud."*
> *(Al-Halabiyyah; al-Sirah, Vol 1, p.274)*

It is this background to Waraqa and the Hebrew Gospel of Matthew that enables us to understand the *Qur'an* at all. For Muhammad, Waraqa was the epitome of *"The people of the Book."*

Abu Talib was the protector and uncle of Muhammad. Whilst living with his uncle, Muhammad finds a job in the business of Khadijah, first cousin of the priest Waraqa. Waraqa immediately believed that God's divine will was for Khadijah and Muhammad to be united together, and declared, *"Oh people of Grace! Let us be witnesses. I am marrying Khadijah, daughter of Khuwaylid, to Muhammad, son of Abdullah."* From this time forward, Waraqa invested his time into Muhammad and they withdrew in solitude in spending one month annually in a cave in Mount Hara for over a 15 year period. (Muslim Sahih, Vol 1, p.78)

For up to 44 years, Muhammad observed Waraqa faithfully translating the Hebrew Gospel of Matthew into Arabic. This translation opened up Muhammad to God's inspired words for mankind. This exposure of Muhammad to translation relates to a misunderstanding that Muhammad was illiterate, which is the common view of the Islamic world today.

The "illiterate," according to the *Qur'an* is referring to the individual or the group who did not own or have knowledge of a Holy Book. Those following the God of Abraham are *People of the Book* (*Ahl Al-Kitab*), whilst the pagan Arabs were *illiterate*. This is why the era of pagan Mecca is referred to as *Jahiliyah*, the Age of Ignorance. The *Qur'an* declares, *"Say to the People of the Book, and to those who are unlearned, 'Do you submit yourselves?"*
(QS 3:20)

Muhammad's vision was for the *illiterate*, which are those who had no knowledge of the book, to become *People of the Book. "*

There is no call on us than to find the path for
the illiterate."
(QS 3:75)

The illiterates are the pagan Arabs, whilst the people of the Book are the children of Isaac and the Christians who had the Gospels.

For Muhammad, divine knowledge came through learning and acquiring truth from the people who read the book before him (QS 10:94). Muhammad regularly had doubts of his own knowledge, and he instructed his followers to ask the people of the Book for advice. This recommendation of Muhammad appears several times in the *Qur'an*.

"Ask the men of Scriptures, if you do not know it." (QS 16:43, QS 21:7) The *Qur'an* is directing the Arab community towards those who are spiritually literate, that is those who have knowledge of the Book.

In all of this background, historians endeavour to disconnect Muhammad's special relationship with Waraqa. However, Waraqa had prepared his student well, and with the passing of Waraqa, Muhammad leads the Nazarene community in Mecca. Waraqa always had a special place in the mind of Muhammad. Muhammad would later say"

> *"You will surely find those closest in love to*
> *the Believers to be those who say, 'we are*
> *Christians.' This is because some of them are*
> *pastors and monks, and they aren't proud."*
> *(QS 5:82)*

Muhammad understood the task that was expected of him. He started to preach to Mecca and to proclaim to the spiritually illiterate. As Waraqa's successor, to avoid excessive elevation of himself, he declared within the *Qur'an*, "I am only a Warner."

His proclamation was a call for Meccan pagans to embrace the Hebrew Gospel of Matthew that was translated by his beloved mentor. Despite the foundations that Waraqa had invested into Muhammad, the death of Waraqa caused all revelation to dry up for nearly three years.

Muhammad had observed his mentor committing his life to the translation of the Book from Hebrew to Arabic. Where does this place the *Qur'an*? The word *Qur'an* refers to a commentary. The final product of the Arabic translation produced by Waraqa was not able to be duplicated like we do with a modern printing press.

> Muhammad declared concerning the *Qur'an*, *"We explain in detail the verses for the people who understand."* (7:32, 9:11) The *Qur'an* expands and elaborates some of the teachings of the Book for the situation in Arabia in the 7th Century. With respect and honour to the task that his mentor worked on, Muhammad declared, *"It is he who sent down to you in truth, the Book confirming what went before it."*
> (QS 3:3)

For Muhammad, he was the itinerant promoter of Waraqa Bin Nauful life's work. Despite Muhammad referring to many as *People of the Book*, minimal copies of Scripture were available. In fact, nearly 1000 years after Muhammad, Scripture was still only available to the clergy. Muhammad expanded on the original Hebrew Gospel for his Arabic listeners, where as far as we know; only one copy existed for hundreds of thousands of Arabic speakers.

In a society that was oral, and had no access to written scripture, the proclamation of Muhammad was a summary of stories, concerning former prophets, events, teachings and parables. In a society that was devoid of written scripture, the motivation of Muhammad was to bring summaries of teaching that was easy to

A journey from extremism to love

recite. This is in fact a central theme of the *Qur'an*.

> *"We have indeed made the Qur'an easy to understand and remember."*
> *(QS 54:17)*

> *"Verily, we have made this Qur'an easy, in your tongue, in order that they may give heed."*
> *(QS 44:58)*

> *"So we have made the Qur'an easy in your own language, that with it you may give glad tidings to the righteous and warnings to people given to contention."*
> *(QS 19:97)*

Although the Hebrew Gospel of Matthew is the foundation for Waraqa and Muhammad's message, it would be incorrect to say that their spiritual foundation was limited to this. There seems to be strong evidence that Muhammad's teaching embraced the Church's oral tradition as well as even Orthodox Christian doctrine that was not compatible with standard Nazarene beliefs. An example of this would be the belief in the Virgin Birth.

Muhammad's revelation did not come from nothing. He endeavoured to declare that his revelation was in unity with existing revelation. Waraqa had formed the paradigm of the Messenger of Islam, so that his declaration would be intended to be grounded in previous revelation. (QS 5:68)

Despite the translation from Hebrew to Arabic by Waraqa, the Hebrew and Arabic revelations are inseparable for Muhammad. The Arabic explains the first, that being the Hebrew Torah and Gospel. The Arabic also refers and directs people to the Hebrew. The Arabic is the witness of the Hebrew. Believers among Arabs were not to elevate Arabic, as it was a witness to the former revelation. Islam today presents the opposite. Those who only believe in the Arabic *Qur'an* follow the tradition of later Islam, and not of Muhammad.

How did Muhammad learn the former revelation, the Torah and the Gospel? There are two alternatives to this question. Firstly, did Muhammad discover the former revelation of scriptures alone, remembering that former revelation being in original Hebrew? Or secondly, Muhammad became familiar with the former revelation through a teacher and guide?

There's no record that Muhammad understood Hebrew, and so the former revelation that he stood for was taught to him.

This was the legacy Waraqa left with Muhammad. Many would feel uneasy about that thought, that Muhammad had a person who instructed him in spiritual truth, however this was the spirit in which Muhammad presented to his followers, as he encouraged them to follow his model, which is asking and learning from the *People of the Book*.

With Waraqa Bin Nauful recognising himself as a part of the Nazarenes, who traced themselves back to the Jewish followers of Way of the Book of Acts, some would declare him as being legalistic, bound to the Torah. Didn't the Nazarenes, who were scattered throughout the region, oppose orthodox theology?

There cannot be certainty of some aspects. Was the Hebrew version of Matthew's gospel described in this section protected and maintained according to the original? Was this the Gospel that was translated by Waraqa Bin Nauful from Hebrew to Arabic and later embraced by Muhammad? As this article has revealed, there is a reasonable case that the original Hebrew version of the Gospel of Matthew was the basis for the Gospel that Muhammad was associated with.

Again, we pursue building a bridge, not the further creation of walls of division.

A journey from extremism to love

Glossary

Hadith	A collection of traditions containing sayings of the prophet Muhammad.
Halal	Food prepared as prescribed by Muslim law
Haram	An Arabic term meaning "forbidden"
Injil	The Arabic name for the New Testament
Jihad	A war or struggle against unbelievers or the spiritual struggle against sin.
Madrasah	An Islamic Boarding School
Quraysh	The ruling tribe of Mecca at the time of the birth of the Prophet Muhammad
Ramadhan	The ninth month of the Muslim year, during which strict fasting is observed
Rotan	Bamboo
Sharia	God's Law according to Islam
Sholat Luhur	Early afternoon Prayers
Sholat Maghrib	Early evening prayer
Sholat Subuh	The early morning Islamic Prayer
Subuh	Dawn

Selected Bibliography

Azzi, J. (2005).   The Priest and the Prophet. Los
                           Angeles: The Pen Publishers.
Bivin, D. (1994).   New Insights from a Hebraic
                           Perspective. Destiny Image Publishers.
Bivin, D. (2005).   New Light on the Difficult Words of
                           Jesus. En-Gedi Resource Centre.
Pritz, R. (1992).   Nazarene Jewish Christianity. Magnes.
Schonfield, H. (2009).   The History of Jewish Christianity.
                           CreateSpace Independent Publishing.
Skarsaune, O. (2007).   Jewish Believers in Jesus: The Early
                           Centuries. Baker Academic.
Trimingham, J. S. (1978). Christianity Amongst the Arabs in Pre-
                           Islamic Times. Longman Group UK.
Watt, W. M. (1993).   Muhammad at Mecca. Kazi Pubns Inc.
Watt, W. M. (1981).   Muhammad at Medina. Oxford
                           University Press.
Watt, W. M. (1974).   Muhammad, Prophet and Statesman.
                           Oxford University Press.